CLIMBING YOUR BEST

Training to Maximize Your Performance

D0973002

0   11557 02735   8

CLIMBING YOUR BEST

Training to Maximize Your Performance

Heather Reynolds Sagar

Photography by Nicholas Sagar

STACKPOLE
BOOKS

Published by
STACKPOLE BOOKS
5067 Ritter Road
Mechanicsburg, PA 17055
www.stackpolebooks.com

Printed in the United States

10 9 8 7 6 5 4 3 2 1

First edition

All photographs by Nicholas Sagar

Cover photo: Tommy Caldwell on Kryptonite

Cover design by Wendy A. Reynolds

Illustrations by Alan Sagar

Page 8   Matt O'Connor on the Onion Boulder, Breckenridge, Colorado.

Page 27   Robby O'Leary looking at a new 5.13 on the Tsunami Wall at the Boulder Rock Club.

Page 79   Tommy Caldwell in Rocky Mountain National Park, Colorado.

Page 111   Nick Sagar on Tomfoolery, Rifle City Park, Colorado.

Page 128   Nick Sagar on Twinkie, Red River Gorge, Kentucky.

Visit the Sagars' website at www.nhclimb.com

Library of Congress Cataloging-in-Publication Data

Sagar, Heather Reynolds.
    Climbing your best : training to maximize your performance / Heather Reynolds Sagar.
        p.   cm.
    Includes bibliographic references (p.) and index.
    ISBN 0-8117-2735-1 (pbk.)
        1. Rock Climbing—Training. I. Title.
GV200.2 .S24   2001
796.52'2—dc21   00-061206

Contents

Exercises, Tables, Forms, etc.

Acknowledgments

There are many people whose support has made this book possible. The most important influence has come from my husband and climbing partner, Nick Sagar. Numerous friends have directly and indirectly offered support and feedback—including Matt and Laura O'Connor, Mike and Kerri Radicella, and their daughters, Jessica and Jennifer. These friends were instrumental in the technical-support realm, not to mention the honesty element. Jim Collins and Jim Logan provided faith and experience. Also, many thanks to Prana, La Sportiva, Clif Bar, Arc'teryx, DMM, and Maxim for the ongoing support of my professional climbing career.

Over the past eight years, my experience with climbers has introduced me to many of the ideas described in this book. Activities and training tips have been accumulated from the experiences of many other climbers. Without their input, this source would be less complete.

To the numerous people who have indirectly influenced this project—from my first climbing partners and friends, university faculty, and clients—thank you. I hope that this tool will enable you to reach your highest endeavors.

Introduction

hrough the years of providing personal training to clients wanting to become
better climbers, I have been asked to describe a typical client. In my experience, typical clients are people who have climbed for a number of years and
feel that their performance has been maintained but has not necessarily improved.
Generally they want more out of their climbing than they have been getting. These
individuals may not wish to win World Cups or even their local bouldering competition, but they do desire to reach the next grade. Mainly, they are frustrated with
climbing at the same level for so long.

Some of the easiest clients to work with are beginners. Most (but not all) beginners have no preconceived idea about how they should move from one hold to another. Given this, it is much easier to teach them the most efficient movements, and
to have them adapt these movements more readily. Friend and client Kerri Radicella began to work with me and Nick from her first days of climbing. Although
Kerri would tire quickly, she worked very hard to apply the concepts of body positioning and movement we continued to stress. After a few months, Kerri started
working on developing the strength and power endurance necessary to improve
her performance. Within eight months of starting, Kerri, who had previously not
been involved in any other upper-body sports, was able to do V2 boulder problems
that were up to twenty-plus moves long.

This book is written with Kerri and many clients in mind. My intention is to
guide every climber—regardless of ability, motivation, or time—through a better understanding of how to more efficiently get to the next level. This book provides a
systematic and methodical approach to assessing your strengths and weaknesses. It
offers structured yet flexible options for "training" efficiently. And most important,
the moral of this story is that if you aren't having fun, you won't do it—so have fun!

Climbing is a rapidly growing sport, spurred on by the introduction of indoor
climbing facilities offering vertical birthday parties and introductory-level classes.
This growth has carried over to the continued development of the competitive level
of sport, with more youth participating and preparing for international-level competition. Climbing is no longer just a recreation—it has developed into a true sport.
To some, it is an extreme sport. But for those involved in sport climbing and bouldering, the only thing really extreme are the moves, usually not the protection or
the risk. With this extreme movement comes the complexity of understanding.

Only in the past four years have sport scientists even touched the physical characteristics of the sport, moving away from a concentration on the mental and physiological aspects of fear and its effect on performance. Since 1991, numerous training
and how-to books have flooded the market. The focus of these books has been to introduce to you ideas on structuring your time and getting stronger. The disadvantage of these sources is that they have provided little flexibility for those who don't

have the time or inclination to "train." These books are based on the experiences of expert climbers and what has worked for them. Unfortunately, this is not all there is to understanding the sport. Coaches must understand biomechanics, physiology, and sport psychology. Their job is to take the individual's talent and nurture it into producing excellent performance. While this is an overwhelming task for a book, and while most of you do not aspire to Olympic-level performance, many concepts can be described and adapted to fit your individual needs. This approach is what separates this book from the other training-related books on the market today.

The easy-to-read approach of this book guides you through understanding your physical and physiological weakness. While reading, you will be guided through a decision-making process of defining what priority climbing performance has for you, what you need to work on, and how to best manage the time committed to climbing so that you can improve while still having fun. The illustrations of techniques may be used to enhance your awareness of movement and balance. The ideas for stretching and strengthening, bringing a better foundation to your general fitness, are ones that will be ever changing as you continue to climb more and more routes. Hopefully, this book will be a helpful resource for you every time you feel a need to refocus on your climbing goals and want to reassess climbing in terms of your life.

In writing this book, it has been my intention to give you new insights into your own performance. My intention is to provide ways to help you efficiently progress to your goals. The first step toward success is to identify the most enjoyable components of this sport and to set appropriate goals. There are many ways to achieve your goals, and these ways can be as flexible or as disciplined as you decide. The trick is to commit to working outside of your comfort zone. With these basic steps, you will improve.

In discussing this project with many friends and climbing partners, I received various responses. Some people were excited about this book, while others felt that the process of climbing should be about having fun and enjoyment, not about work. This resource can be used with a minimum amount of structure or a maximum level of organization. The choice is yours. It is also your responsibility to identify how you respond to the structure you outline. With this self-discovery, you can increase your potential by giving yourself more of what you want and by filtering out what you don't like.

It is a challenge to credit all those who provide insight and ideas on training. Many ideas and practices are learned in the gym from watching someone else and then trying it. Tips can be picked up in training-related articles in *Climbing* or *Rock & Ice.* I hope that this book will help you to take the things that you have been doing and use them more effectively. Or perhaps you will gain a better idea of how to manage your climbing time. Better yet, perhaps you will be really motivated to get out there and try your hardest.

Whatever the case, I hope that this resource provides you with many new and exciting ideas to take to the crag or the gym. We will not all become 5.14 climbers, but we can all become better climbers. Use this book when you feel that plateau in performance or that lack of motivation. Pick it up to remind you that climbing is about the process of sending a route, not about the outcome. And finally, remember that if climbing is something you love to do, you will do it well.

Chapter 1

THE PHYSIOLOGY OF CLIMBING

A number of variables determine how the body will respond to the various stresses of climbing—the nature of the work, your personal level of fitness and strength, your flexibility and mental tenacity. For example, *Super Tweak*, a well-known 5.14b in Logan Canyon, Utah, begins with a V9 boulder problem (the first several hand moves are 5.13+ in their own right), continues with 5.13c climbing to a good rest, and concludes with a V8–V9 finishing crux. For Nick Sagar, the powerful crux of the route was the determining factor in success or failure during his redpoint attempts. For Tommy Caldwell, it was the power endurance at the finish. The recovery Nick gained in the rest before the last boulder problem was sufficient for him to get enough juice back to continue to the anchors without fail, though it was not the same for Tommy. While both eventually succeeded in redpointing the route, each climber had to approach it differently according to his personal strengths.

The physiological demands on a climber's body can be classified under the general categories of power, power endurance, recovery, stamina, and endurance.

POWER

Power involves maximum muscle recruitment—the maximum amount of muscle cells you can contract simultaneously to produce a short, fast burst of strength. An example is when a weight lifter summons all his or her power for a maximum lift. Increasing your power requires improving the ability to recruit a maximum number of muscle fibers to work as a unit. This, in turn, involves a coordination of the neurological messages from the brain to the muscle cells about the speed and power of the contraction needed for the move. The muscle fibers respond as a bundle to these messages, generating the power for contraction. If the messages are not coordinated, the muscle bundles fire at different times with insufficient strength to reach the next handhold. Thus, power failures normally cause falls during a move, not while hanging onto the holds.

Your physical strength is determined by two factors: your muscle-fiber type and the amount and type of training you do. Muscle fibers are determined by your genes. There are three types: slow twitch, fast twitch, and a fiber with a combination of both. All three types have varied distribution in muscles. Sport scientists continue to debate the effect of training on the distribution of different fibers. Some studies have shown that training can change fibers (either improving oxygen transport or speed of contraction), resulting in enhanced performance; other studies have shown no change in the fibers. In any case, you may not have the same muscle fibers as the next climber, and therefore may require a different approach to training.

Interestingly, you don't always fail because the muscles didn't create sufficient energy. Sometimes failure is the result of the stretch reflex. If the tension created is greater than the muscle has ever experienced, this reflex will interrupt the brain messages that induce the contraction, causing the muscle to relax. You may have experienced this if you have tried moving heavy furniture or appliances and nothing happened. The stretch reflex is a safety mechanism, designed to prevent the muscle from being overstressed and tearing under the strain of the contraction. If you try the move again immediately, you run a greater risk of injury, because this reflex needs time to recharge before firing again. Rest during power training is therefore crucial.

Unlike lower-intensity moves, multiple power moves are fueled by the anaerobic system of energy—more specifically, the creatine phosphate system. That is, the energy for power moves is not obtained from oxygen delivery to the muscle, but from the chemical breakdown of creatine phosphate stores in the muscle.

POWER ENDURANCE

Power endurance involves more movements at a lower level of intensity than plain power moves do. Power endurance, like power, also includes the anaerobic energy system, but specifically the lactic acid system. Power endurance can be called upon in as few as twenty moves or as many as 100. The easiest way to know if you are taxing your power endurance is if you experience a pump. If you fall with hands opening uncontrollably on the holds and your forearms feeling as though they were going to explode, you are pumped. Physiologically, you have reached the anaerobic threshold, the point at which metabolism has switched from aerobic to anaerobic and your oxygen debt is too high to continue.

You can improve your anaerobic threshold through training both aerobically and anaerobically. Aerobic training involves maintaining a heart rate of 50 to 80 percent of your maximum for twenty minutes or longer. (Fit people will be closer to 80 percent, unfit closer to 50 percent.) Many routes don't take this minimum twenty minutes to climb, and thus you are into recovery before you reap the full benefits of increasing your heart rate. Also, in high-intensity work such as bouldering, redpointing, or on-sight climbs, your heart rate may exceed the recommended 80 percent. In this case, most of the work you do is anaerobic. Anaerobic training involves higher-intensity work for a shorter duration.

High and Low Levels of Power Endurance

Power endurance covers a wide range of movement difficulty over varying periods of time. Low-level power-endurance climbing includes routes well below the on-sight level of the climber, but with continuously moderate moves adding up to a big pump. High-level power endurance includes those short, four-bolt projects that spit you off with pulsing forearms in 30 feet of movement while trying to redpoint.

You benefit most by training at both levels of power endurance. Working below the on-sight and above the redpoint level provides opportunities for working on your aerobic capacity, your anaerobic threshold, and your ability to recover from muscle and energy depletion.

RECOVERY

Recovery refers to the body's ability to diminish the physiological effects of fatigue. The more quickly the climber accomplishes this, the sooner optimum performance levels can be resumed. At some point, the climber will have to rest, but the trick is to minimize the amount of downtime before returning to good performances. Alan Watts of Northern Michigan University showed that it takes a climber an average of twenty minutes of rest to recover from a failure-induced pump. Improving your ability to recover involves practice. Climb on difficult terrain, and then move to easier terrain to rest and flush out the pump.

Recovery can be accomplished both while climbing and while resting. While you belay your partner or grab a bite to eat, you are replenishing your oxygen debt and recovering from your work on the route. Recovery on the route is also possible by those with the ability to find good rest positions and take advantage of them.

STAMINA

Stamina is the amount of continued recovery you can manage throughout a day of climbing. You can roughly quantify your level of stamina by counting the number of pitches and the difficulty of the routes on your on-sight and redpoint attempts. For example, you may have the stamina to do two warm-up routes, three tries on a redpoint project, and then be so tired you can't untie your shoes. Or conversely, you may warm up and do five tries at the redpoint level and then four pitches just below your on-sight, but by then it's too dark to see the holds, and you've no choice but to go home and finish up tomorrow. In the first case, your stamina is low. In the second, it's extremely high.

ENDURANCE

Endurance (not to be confused with power endurance) involves the ability to do numerous low-intensity moves for a long duration without experiencing a pump. Such activity is supported by the climber's cardiovascular system and fueled by aerobic energy: sufficient oxygen is continuously supplied to the muscle to fuel the work, and the work is shared throughout the various muscle bundles. The benefit is a continuous, uninterrupted flow of oxygen through the muscle with no by-products to create fatigue. Hence, no pump occurs.

The maximum volume of oxygen the lungs can hold, known as the VO_2 max, can limit physical exertion. This volume increases with aerobic training and is closely related to the anaerobic threshold; hence, training one element will directly affect another.

Other benefits of aerobic training include an increase in the capillarization of the muscle tissue, allowing better blood supply and improved oxygenation of muscle tissue during work. Endurance work is also touted by many sport scientists as the best way to burn fat as a source for energy.

Endurance work is one of several approaches you can take to improve your VO_2 max and your anaerobic threshold. Specific methods are discussed in more detail in chapter 5.

Keep in mind that there are no strictly defined lines between the physiological categories outlined in this chapter; they operate on a continuum. For example, endurance is aerobic until fatigue—caused by time or the difficulty of moves—makes it anaerobic, and you begin tapping your power endurance. On the other end of the spectrum, power involves maximum effort for one move, but as the climb proceeds and requires more, easier moves, you likewise convert to power endurance.

Chapter 2

ASSESSING PERSONAL STRENGTHS AND WEAKNESSES

*I*n every sport, athletes progress through a series of fitness levels as they continue to excel. Runners will begin at a slower pace and fewer miles and progress to a quicker rate for greater distances. In climbing, the biggest difference is that the required work uses muscle that people have not typically used in other activities, although with the increased popularity of mountain biking, more people approach climbing with better grip strength. The following is a series of physical tests that can be performed at home and at your local gym. The results can be helpful in outlining your strengths and weaknesses.

YOUR STRENGTHS VERSUS THE NATURE OF THE ROUTE

There is a very popular route in Rifle, Colorado, called *Pump-o-rama*. The grade is 5.13a and the route is very power endurance oriented. Most climbers fail due to a continuous pump in the forearms that eventually forces their hands from the holds and leaves their bodies swinging into the Arsenal parking area. Often on a summer weekend evening, the Arsenal parking area fills with people who have come to watch as climbers "warm down" on *Pump-o-rama,* most taking some big air in the process. Watching these climbers who have climbed it many times since their initial redpoint is a treat. You can watch as climbers get countless knee bars and recover on the various sections of the route. It becomes painfully clear that if you have trouble with your power endurance and your knee bars, this route may be more than a bit of a problem for you.

This gives you insight regarding your strategy in attempting to flash, on-sight, or redpoint routes. With the knowledge of your personal strengths and weaknesses, you will have the ability to approach a route with the style that suits your individual strengths. This increases your chance for success. Bouldering partner and friend Matt O'Connor, the manager of the Boulder Rock Club in Boulder, Colorado, illustrates this concept well. Matt is a notoriously slow climber. A still shot of Matt on a route is a fine video performance; at least that's almost true. If Matt tries to speed up, he cannot be as precise with his feet as he is when climbing at his regular pace. The result is that he would fall off because his feet would skate out from under him. While climbing slowly may cause Matt to have to stave off the pump, he can be more precise with his feet—leading to the conclusion that power endurance is probably not a weak link

for Matt, but foot precision could be when he moves quickly.

The trick to determining the secrets of a particular route—such as whether there is a ledge you can lie down on or whether the route is pumpy or has a powerful crux—is to ask others who have done the route. You can then compare their ideas with their strengths and help predetermine your performance. For example, with *Pump-o-rama*, falling at the same point doesn't necessarily mean that the move is difficult—it could mean that at that particular point, your pump gets so great that you can't hang on anymore. Even getting to the knee-bar rest and staying there doesn't mean you'll recover; you may get really pumped again as soon as you resume climbing.

To determine your weak link, use the tests in this chapter to help you gain a better understanding of where your fitness is. Also consider the routes you have climbed. Think about where you've had problems on these routes, as well as where it seemed really easy for you. Getting other climbers' opinions on routes also helps you to better understand the route and yourself by comparison. These tests can also be repeated in the future to help you assess your physical improvement. Bear in mind that physical ability does not necessarily mean you will succeed—there are also the elements of mental strength and technique influencing your performance. **Knowing why you fail is crucial to putting an end to falling and to start sending.**

PHYSICAL CHARACTERISTICS PERTINENT TO PERFORMANCE

As most climbers expect, grip strength relative to body weight is a very important predictor of climbing performance. Sport scientists—including Phil Watts, Russum, Wakasa, and Reynolds—have all noted grip-strength-to-weight ratio as a predictor of climbing performance. These are not the sole predictors of performance, however. Back strength, abdominal strength, body fat, and flexibility are also contributors to performance. If you rely solely on grip strength, you will obviously excel on some routes and fail miserably on others. The best compromise is to be well rounded in your strengths, opening up the options of numerous ways to do the same move.

You possess more strength in some areas than others, and typically use these strengths in your climbing, thus defining your style. For example, some climbers can grab a hold and lock it off at their waist, letting their feet come off as they campus their way up the route. This approach is impossible for others, who tend to rely on pushing upward through the legs and using opposition to move upward. For this reason, some climbers perform better on some routes than other climbers do.

Because route setters, or the first ascensionists, determine the direction and, to a limited extent, the moves of a route, the routes developed will usually suit some people more than others. The climbers who come along and then do the second, third, and fourth ascent often confirm or dispute the grade, but due to the subjectivity of climbing and individual styles, grades really become simply a guideline to use in describing the route. With a better understanding of your style, strengths, and weaknesses, you can better select routes to improve your overall performance or you can chose routes that will be easier for you, thus progressing through grades more quickly.

Some physical traits have a greater influence on performance than others do. For example, grip-strength-to-weight ratio and back-and-shoulder-strength-to-weight ratios show a more significant relationship to performance than does flexibility in the hip. However, flexibility is a better predictor of climbing performance than is leg power. The following tests are designed to allow you to assess your physical strengths and handicaps. Use the form at the end of the chapter to record your information for comparison to the tables at the end of the chapter. It is best to complete these tests when you have had at least twenty-four to thirty-six hours of rest from climbing or other activities. Follow the tests in the order outlined, choosing with the grip- and back-strength tests one of the two alternatives. You may also need the assistance of a partner for many of the tests.

Characteristics pertinent to climbing performance include: grip strength, back and shoulder strength, abdominal strength, flexibility, and VO$_2$ max. Imbalances in strength can increase your potential for injury.

TEST 1	**OPEN-HAND GRIP STRENGTH**

Equipment:
Hangboard or like holds that are one and a half to two pads in an open-hand position on an edge.
Bathroom scale.
Stopwatch.
Directions:
Stand on the scale (for best results, use the same scale for measuring body weight as you use in this test). With both hands, grip the holds on the hangboard and try to take as much weight as possible off the scale without bending your elbows. The recorder times the average scale weight over five seconds.
Example:
Use the following equation to determine the percentage of body weight you held.
% Body weight held = 1 – (weight on scale in lbs./body weight in lbs.)
% Body weight held = 1 – (20 lbs./115 lbs.)
The scale measured 20 lbs. Your body weight is 115 lbs. That means you held the remaining 95 lbs. (115 lbs. – 20 lbs. = 95 lbs.)
=1 – (0.174)
= 0.826
The weight on the scale is 17.4% of 115. The weight off the scale is 82.6% of 115, your body weight. Thus, you held 82.6% of your body weight. Your grip-strength-to-weight ratio is 0.826.

TEST 2	GRIP STRENGTH

Equipment:
Nautilus machine (or equivalent).
Carabiner or bar with attachment for machine.
Directions:
Using the weight unit for leg lifts or biceps curls, attach the carabiner or bar to the
machine. Using table 1 at the end of the chapter, select the most appropriate
weight listed and set that on the machine. Lie on the floor, parallel to the machine. With the arm fully extended, grasp the carabiner in the tips of the fingers.
Have your partner brace your body at the upper chest by sitting next to it. Curl the
fingers into the palm, being careful not to pull with the biceps or body away
from the Nautilus machine. If you can lift this weight, increase the weight by 5
pounds and repeat the exercise after a fifteen-minute rest. If you need to try more
than four times with added rest, better to try this test again after resting twenty-
four to forty-eight hours, starting with the last weight successfully lifted.
Complete this test for the opposite hand as well. Record the heaviest weight you
successfully lift with the fingers.
Notes:
As a partner on this test, be certain to hold the elbow, ensuring that it is not incorporated into the pull of the fingers.
Provide enough support against the upper body of the tester to resist body movement toward the machine.
Start the test with fingers fully extended and resisting the pull of the weights.
Use the number of pounds pulled with the forearm muscles isolated. This number
is divided by your body weight to give you a ratio. The ratio can be outlined on
the form and used in assessing grip-strength-to-weight ratio from the tables at
the end of the chapter.
Example:
Pounds pulled = 84 on the right and 86 on the left. The average equals 85. Your
body weight equals 138. Therefore, 85/138 = 0.616. Your grip-strength-to-weight
ratio is 0.616. If you are female, this is close to the average for a 5.10 or easy 5.11
climber. If you are a male, this number indicates a 5.8/5.9 performance level. If
the climber climbs 5.12, then he or she has a grip-strength-to-weight weakness.
This could potentially lead to injury if the back strength is in the 5.12 range. Ultimately, working on the grip strength specifically could help this climber perform better.

TEST 3	BACK AND SHOULDER STRENGTH

Equipment:
Nautilus machine (or equivalent).
Harness and sling.
Pull-up bar.

Directions:
Using the lat pull-down aspect of the Nautilus equipment, stand facing the machine. Using the sling and harness, anchor the tester to the base of the machine, allowing no or little upward movement of the tester. Note that some machines have a system where the tester can sit, putting his or her knees under a brace. This will also work.

Hold the pull-up bar, palms facing away from yourself, shoulder-width apart. Using table 1, select the appropriate weight to initiate the test, and attempt to pull the weight past the eyes, in front of the face. Due to the anchor system, you should be able to bend the elbows only to ninety degrees. If this pull is not done, decrease the weight in 5-pound increments until a successful pull is accomplished, resting fifteen minutes between tries. Similarly, if this pull is easily done, increase the weight by 5-pound increments, resting ten to twelve minutes between tries, and continue until the user fails to pull the bar down.

Notes:
Too many attempts will cause fatigue that can affect the results. If you must repeat pulls more than six times, rest twenty-four to forty-eight hours before trying this test again, starting with the weight closest to success.

If the anchor is not snug enough and you pull the weight lower than suggested, you are using more muscles than desired in this test. Tighten the anchor. Ensure that you place hands shoulder-width apart on the bar.

Feet can come off the ground in this test.

The number of pounds registered on the scale is then divided by body mass to get a back-and-shoulder-strength-to-weight ratio for the subject.

Example:
You pull 289 pounds on the machine. The weight is 140. The back-and-shoulder-strength-to-weight ratio equals 289/140, or 2.06. This ratio can then be compared to the tables at the end of the chapter. For males or females, this number would indicate very high strength-to-weight ratio, predicting a performance level of 5.13 or better. If you compare this to your grip-strength-to-weight ratio and get a dramatic difference, I would suggest you work on grip strength in order to prevent injury. Likewise, if the number is in the range of your performance level, this is a strength rather than a weakness.

TEST 4	BACK AND SHOULDER STRENGTH

Equipment:

Free weights.

Harness and sling.

Pull-up bar.

Directions:

Wearing the harness, attach the appropriate amount of weights. Use table 1 to determine the amount. The total weight should equal the percentage of body weight listed in the table. You then attempt to do a pull-up with the weight attached. If you fail do a pull-up, reduce the weight on the harness by 5 pounds and repeat the process until you do one pull-up. If you easily complete the pull, then add weight in 5-pound increments until you fail to do a pull-up.

Notes:

If more than four pulls are required fatigue will affect the results. It would be better to retest at a future time.

Use a static pull rather than a dynamic pull in the test. Rest fifteen minutes between each pull with added or diminished weight.

Example:

The greatest amount of weight pulled before failure is the amount used in the equation. If you completed the pull-up with 60 pounds, then add your weight. For example: 108 pounds + 60 pounds = 168 pounds. Then use the total pounds in the pull-up (168) and divide by your body weight (108). 168/108 = 1.56. This is the ratio that you compare to the tables at the end of the chapter. For both male and female climbers, this would indicate an expected performance level of 5.11. If you climb at a higher standard, this is considered a physical weakness. If the opposite is true, you may be a strong technical climber but need to improve your back strength.

TEST 5	ABDOMINAL STRENGTH

Equipment:

Watch.

Pad on the floor.

Directions:

In the traditional sit-up position (hands behind the head, knees bent), with a partner holding your feet, do as many complete sit-ups (from shoulders on the ground to elbows touching knees) as possible in one minute. You should reach failure at the end of the minute. Compare your results to table 3 on page 17.

Notes:

You must complete each sit-up for it to count.

The hands must stay behind the head.

During this test, it is important to keep your back flat against the floor or mat. Do not lift your hips to assist in the sit-up action.

TEST 6	**SIT & REACH**

Equipment:
Two rulers.
Directions:
Sit with your back directly against a wall, with legs extended out in front. Have a partner place both rulers at your right heel, with one ruler pointing out from your heel and the other toward your knee. Then reach with fingers outstretched toward your toes, passing them if possible. The partner measures the distance between the tip of the middle right finger and the right heel. If the tip does not reach the heel, record the number with a minus sign in front; if past the heel, record as a positive number. Compare your results to those listed in table 2 or 3.

TEST 7	**FLEXION**

Equipment:
Protractor.
Pencil.
Directions:
Stand next to a wall, with straight legs and arms at the side. Use the pencil to mark a point on the wall where the leg bends at the hip. Then mark the knee. Draw a straight line between the two. With back straight and outside leg remaining straight, lift the inside leg up, with a bent knee, as high as possible. The partner now marks the position of the knee. Move away from the wall and your partner, using the protractor, draws a line between the starting position of the hip and the final knee position. Line up the protractor with zero degrees along the standing position and measure the angle change from the starting position to the finish position.
Notes:
The outside leg and back should remain straight during the action.
Repeat this test for both legs.
Do not assist the lift of the leg with your hands.
Results are outlined in tables 2 and 3 for women and men, respectively.

TEST 8	**STAMINA**

Requirements:
Route that you have done at your on-sight level.
Patient belayer.
Directions:
Climb laps on the route, with no rest between. Do not down climb the route. Quickly lower to the ground and repeat the route until failure. You must not have a rest position where you spend time depumping (recovering)—this is a continuous-climbing test. Record the number of successful laps, not the lap where you failed.
Results are outlined in table 4 at the end of the chapter. There are no differences for men and women in scoring on these tests.

TEST 9   POWER

Requirements:
Route or boulder problem three grades harder than your hardest redpoint. You need only try a route of six to eight moves or a section of a route in that many moves.
Belayer or spotter.

Directions:
Try this problem five to fifteen times per day over four days. Make sure you give it only five tries before taking fifteen to twenty minutes' rest. Give the problem a maximum total of thirty tries over four days of climbing. Record whether you have success or not, and when success occurred. You do not need to continue to try the problem after success. Compare your results to those outlined in table 4 at the end of this chapter.

TEST 10   RECOVERY

Requirements:
Route between the on-sight and redpoint level—one that the climber can successfully climb.
Route three grades below the on-sight level—one that the climber is familiar with.
Patient belayer.

Directions:
Warm up well and rest twenty minutes from last warm-up route. Climb a difficult route, followed by an easier route without any rest between tries. Repeat both the easy and difficult routes, again without resting. Record whether you successfully completed all routes or when you fell. The results for comparison are outlined in table 4 at the end of the chapter.

TEST 11   PACE

Requirements:
Stopwatch or timer.
Route of twenty-four to thirty hand moves at the on-sight level—one that you have never done before.
Route at the on-sight level, with twenty-four to thirty hand moves—one that you have done before.
Redpoint project of twenty-four to thirty moves.
Belayer and timekeeper.

Directions:
Attempt all of these routes while the timekeeper keeps track of your time for each ascent. You can have as much rest as required between each attempt. The timekeeper stops the clock when you fall and begins timing again when you resume climbing. Record the total time it takes you to do the route, minus time hanging on the rope. This time should include clipping the anchors. Use table 4 in this chapter for comparison of results.

THE RESULTS

Your test results can now be compared to the table provided at the end of the chapter. The first seven tests can be compared numerically to the values in tables 2 and 3. While making the comparisons, bear in mind that evidence suggests that some climbing areas and gyms can promote specific strengths. Tables 2 and 3 contain average values for men and women across North America. While examining the tables, bear in mind that the 5.13 and 5.14 climbers' values have a smaller range of variance than at the grades below this level. This means that the scores for 5.13 and 5.14 climbers are very close together, whereas the scores for 5.11 and 5.12 climbers, for example, may vary greatly. One 5.12a redpoint climber may have a grip-strength-to-weight ratio of 0.89, while another has 0.64. If you are a 5.13+ or 5.14 climber, use the numbers indicated in the table under the 5.13 category as the lowest possible score you should have. In other words, your scores should be higher than those indicated.

FORM 1	PERSONAL RESULTS			
Date:	Name:			
Age:	Weight:		Height:	
Redpoint outside:		On-sight	outside:	Traditional
inside:			inside:	Sport
Bouldering grade				
Grip strength	Test 1	% of body weight:		
	Test 2	lbs.:		
	Ratio = grip lbs. from Test 2/Body weight:			
Back and shoulder strength	Test 1	lbs.:		
	Test 2	% of body weight:		
Abdominal strength	Number of sit-ups per minute:			
Reach	+ or –	inches		
Flexion	Right leg: degrees		Left leg: degrees	
Stamina	Number of laps:		Grade of route:	
Recovery				
Power				
Pace	New on-sight:		seconds	
	On-sight level:		seconds	
	Redpoint try:		seconds	

TABLE 1   SUGGESTED WEIGHTS FOR TESTS 2 TO 4

Table 1 can be used to assist you in determining the appropriate weight with which to begin the test if you have no previous experience with free weights. These are merely suggestions, and you need to adjust the weight according to your personal fitness. If you begin with a weight that is too heavy, you may have to delay the test until you have had twenty-four hours to recover. If you select a weight that is much too light, increase the weight by more than 5 pounds and repeat your attempt. If you have to increase the weight more than six to eight times, again you may have to delay completion of the test until you have had twenty-four hours' recovery time.

Climbing Grade		Grip Weight	Back and Shoulder Weight
5.8/9	women	60–65% of body weight	125–140% of body weight
	men	60–65% of body weight	160–170% of body weight
5.10	women	60–70% of body weight	150–155% of body weight
	men	65–75% of body weight	170–180% of body weight
5.11	women	70–80% of body weight	150–160% of body weight
	men	70–80% of body weight	175–190% of body weight
5.12	women	75–85% of body weight	160–180% of body weight
	men	75–85% of body weight	185–200% of body weight
5.13	women	80–90% of body weight	175–190% of body weight
	men	85–90% of body weight	195–205% of body weight
5.14	women	95–100% of body weight	185–200% of body weight
	men	95–100% of body weight	200% or more of body weight

Tables 2 and 3: Comparative Results for Strength and Flexibility
The following are the tables for comparison of results collected and reported in form 1. Remember that these values are a suggested minimum for the given test. If you score lower than the value indicated, this could be considered a physical weakness you need to improve.

TABLE 2   TARGET SCORES FOR WOMEN

Grade	Sit-Ups	Grip	Back	Reach	Flexion
Up to 5.10	Up to 35	Up to 0.65	1.3–1.50	Up to +5	Up to 120
5.11–5.12	35–45	0.65–0.80	1.50–1.85	+6 to +7	120 to130
5.13a & up	45 & up	0.80 & up	1.78 & up	+7 & up	130 & up

TABLE 3		TARGET SCORES FOR MEN			
Grade	Sit-ups	Grip	Back	Reach	Flexion
Up to 5.10	Up to 42	Up to 0.70	1.6–1.80	Up to +3	Up to 120
5.11a–5.12	42–44	0.70–0.85	1.8–1.95	+4– +5	120–125
5.13	46 & up	0.85 & up	1.95 & up	+4 & up	125 & up
5.14	48 & up	0.95 & up	2.2 & up	+4 & up	125 & up

Data for tables 1–3 collected by Heather Reynolds Sagar between 1994 and 1999.

Note: The above scores are based on averages for climbers of the grades listed based on redpoint grade. If you do not redpoint four letter grades harder than you on-sight, look at scores that are four grades above your on-sight. If you redpoint more than four grades harder than your on-sight, look at your redpoint grade category.

TABLE 4	DESIRED RESULTS OF PHYSIOLOGICAL TESTS		
Stamina	Power	Recovery	Pace
For this test, you should complete at least two laps on a route two letter grades below your on-sight level.	You should be able to do a boulder problem three letter grades more difficult than the hardest redpoint grade you can successfully accomplish.	During this interval test, you should be able to successfully do the hard/easy route pattern twice with less than 3 minutes' rest.	On the on-sight, your time should be under 210 seconds. On a rehearsed route, under 150 seconds. On a redpoint project, under 180 seconds, assuming there is a rest position on the route.

After studying your scores, you'll know specifically what you need to focus on. So how do you do it? Chapter 5 outlines workouts geared toward working the elements—for example, recovery, power endurance, and power. If you have discovered a specific strength or flexibility problem, use table 4 as a guide to find the specific exercises to help you eliminate this personal weakness.

Use the exercises outlined in chapter 5 to work on a specific physiological weakness such as recovery or power. Use the specific exercises for strength outlined in chapter 4 to work on a movement pattern as well as a physical weakness.

PHYSIOLOGICAL FOUNDATION

An imbalance in muscle strength between opposing-muscle groups and upper arm and lower arm can increase your potential for injury. One previous client experienced a great deal of elbow tendonitis. Closer examination illustrated an imbalance in the strength of his upper arm relative to his forearm. If you notice a discrepancy in the grade and strength values, you may wish to develop some strength in the weak link.

As with strength, physiological factors have a balance as well. Use the following descriptions as a guide to assist you in determining your strengths and weaknesses physiologically. When interpreting this information, bear in mind that the descriptions are for routes at your limit. This means the most difficult routes you could accomplish with a redpoint format or on an on-sight try. Let's look at a sample ideal grade distribution.

Power (hardest moves you can do)	11d (V2)
Redpoint (hardest route you can do within ten days of working it)	11a
On-sight (best on-sight and with low consistency)	10a
Stamina (you can barely complete three laps)	5.9
Endurance (aerobic climbing for twenty to thirty minutes)	5.6 or 5.7

DESCRIPTION OF LEVELS

Bouldering (power) level = Your power level should be achievable within ten days of work, and the grade should be three letter grades above your redpoint level in comparison with the Yosemite decimal rating system.

Redpoint level = The redpoint limit should be done in ten climbing days. The grade is optimally three letter grades below power level and four letter grades higher than on-sight level.

On-sight level = An on-sight grade ideally reflects the hardest route accomplished given six to eight tries at this grade. The grade should be a full number grade below redpoint level and two letter grades above stamina level.

Stamina level = Ideally, this grade is two letter grades below on-sight level and/or three letter grades above endurance level. Refer to the stamina test in this chapter.

Endurance level = Conceivably, this level is three grades below stamina level and/or five letter grades below on-sight level. You do not get pumped at this level.

Pace = Results for the pace tests vary according to height of routes. For a practiced on-sight or redpoint, your time should be at most 140 seconds for approximately thirty moves.

THE GRADE PYRAMID

This sample pyramid for a 5.13– climber demonstrates the distribution of grades for relative redpoint and on-sight levels. Regardless of the grade you currently redpoint and on-sight, you can adapt a similar pattern.

5.13a						Redpoint limit
5.12d	5.12d	5.12d				
5.12c	5.12c	5.12c	5.12c			
5.12b	5.12b	5.12b	5.12b	5.12b		
5.12a	5.12a	5.12a	5.12a	5.12a	5.12a	On-sight limit

It gets tricky when you are dealing with grades below 5.10 because these are not distinguished with letter grades. Use the following pyramid as a guide. Note that the plus indicates a harder route, and the minus sign reflects an easier route.

5.9							Redpoint limit
5.9 –	5.9 –						
5.8 –	5.8+	5.9	5.8+	5.8 –			
5.7	5.7	5.8 –	5.8 –	5.7	5.7		
5.7	5.7	5.7	5.6	5.6	5.6	5.6	On-sight limit

Chapter 3

DETERMINING AND PRIORITIZING WEAKNESSES

With a clear understanding of the elements that negatively affect your climbing performance, you need to relate these elements to your overall goals, likes, and dislikes within the sport. The key is to keep climbing fun while you're working on what consistently gives you problems. Use the information in this chapter to again assess your approach to climbing and training. Keeping all aspects of climbing in mind, determine what you like the most about the sport. Is it the success of doing a hard redpoint or the thrill of running it out? Maybe your greatest enjoyment is in winning competitions. Maybe you prefer to focus on the physical demands of the sport. Do you like getting pumped? Or do you like placing your foot by your hand and rocking onto it while you slap with one hand to the next hold a mile away?

SORTING THROUGH THE WEAKNESSES

Climbers' first trip to Rifle, Colorado, often leaves them feeling pretty discouraged and slapped around. The reason is simple. The grades aren't more difficult than elsewhere, but the nature of the body positions and movement required are unique. Many routes—such as *The Rehabilitator* (5.11c)—follow sloping holds on big blocks. This particular route is actually an almost vertical face, and it can feel like 5.12a. The interesting thing about *The Rehabilitator* is that it requires you to get pretty extended, especially if you're shorter than most climbers. In Rifle, it is much more difficult to climb in general, if you make small moves and try to bring your feet up to lock holds at your shoulder. Conversely, you need to stay low on these sloping holds, bring your feet high, arch away from the handhold, rather than pull it in, and reach really high for the next hold. Getting a good rest position demands techniques such as heel/toe cams, knee bars or scums, and even turning your body away from the rock. If you aren't well versed in this type of climbing, Rifle can be a mortifying place to climb.

Climbing in areas that do not suit your style can be a lesson in frustration, but it can also help you to prioritize your training approach. Rifle has a reputation as a very difficult area. However, for those of you who climb well in the gym and use tricks such as knee bars and heel/toe cams, climbing in Rifle is fun at any grade. Conversely, Rifle can be intimidating and confusing, simply because it favors the climber who makes big moves and uses body position rather than brute strength and a more direct approach. The point is, if you are bad at recovery on a route and you want to be better at it, Rifle is the kind of area that will force you to work on this. You will fail a lot initially, but success will come. Continued success does not allow you to see your weaknesses, and therefore success on harder things can be more difficult to attain. Failure teaches you what to work on and how to do it. Without failing, it is harder to learn.

The difficulty for most people in determining their weaknesses and strengths is a lack of understanding of how to relate the failures to a particular weakness. Did you fall because you were pumped, or did your foot skid off? Or did your foot skid off because you were pumped and pulling in too much? If you fell because you were pumped, it might be a lack of power endurance or the ability to recover. If the fall was the result of the foot skating, it may be more an issue of foot placement or core tension, pushing through the foot effectively. The later may be a result of both core tension and the precision with the foot.

One of the tricks to resolving this problem is to spend some time bouldering, where everything except a low end of power endurance and endurance are exaggerated. If your foot continually comes off on more-vertical problems as well as steeper things, then chances are pretty good that it's an issue of footwork. On the other hand, if you can't seem to do forty moves at your redpoint level because you're pumped, though you can do sections of the route without a problem, then it might just be your recovery on route.

Working on powerful problems gives you the opportunity to fall and immediately ask yourself, "Why did I fall?" Initially, you may have trouble identifying the exact reason, or any reason. But eventually it becomes easier and easier to say, "I fell because my foot came off—I need to push more through the left foot." You have just learned something about your body tension—it wasn't adequate to execute the move. The push through the foot is a subtle part of the required tension through the core. Now that you know this, you can work on it.

In a different case, you may not be able to reach or latch the next hold. Why? Is it because you didn't get enough height? Maybe it's because your contact strength isn't great. Or was it because your body position didn't let you hang onto it? In an attempt to answer that question, you need to examine each of those questions more closely. Identifying the right answers to these questions enables you to make the appropriate change.

The following list of signs of weakness can be used as a guide in analyzing whether particular weaknesses are having a negative effect on your current performance. You can take this one step further and examine what you will need to be really proficient in your quest to accomplish your performance goals. For example, you want to free a big wall, such as *The Nose*. You know by the grades of the pitches that you will need to have great stamina at the 5.12 level, as well as good crack-climbing and face-climbing technique. More than likely, you won't need to be really proficient on steeper stuff. However, you will have to be able to do a pitch or two of 5.13-mid climbing with fatigue. You can even determine how much finger strength versus back and arm strength you will need, and train appropriately. Basically, you approach it with a strategy.

Even if your goal is not as far-reaching, you can learn about the route and the angle, particular crux sections. Your training may be more inclusive, helping you to succeed on numerous routes as well as that one. When you are using the following guide of symptom versus potential weakness, think about your weaknesses in terms of your goals, and factor in the type of climbing you prefer. If you think it may adversely affect your future goals, then you list these shortcomings in order of their importance. First, determine which appears to have the highest detrimental effect and give it a high priority in your climbing program or schedule. Second, select a second-highest problem and train for it, but perhaps less frequently. Or, as you experience improvement in one area, move to another area. For example, if one fault is poor technique on steeper terrain, start working on steeper routes, even if they are a little easier for you. As you become more comfortable climbing on steep rock and you see more success, stay on the steeper terrain and start focusing on a second flaw, such as foot precision. Climb steeper routes with smaller footholds.

Weakness	Signs & Symptoms
Low grip strength	• You tend to always bend your arms. • You find that grabbing the rope to clip is taxing. • You have difficulty dead-hanging small holds.
Poor contact strength	• You can make the move to the hold, but have difficulty latching the hold. • You can hang the same hold you have trouble latching.
Low back strength	• You have difficulty doing big moves.
Low upper-arm strength	• You have difficulty locking holds off.
Low core strength	• You have difficulty climbing with one foot on and extended away from you. • You have trouble gaining control if you swing off a route. • You have trouble keeping feet on holds on steep terrain. • You may experience low-back pain. • You may have a strong back and upper arms. • You forget how to do sit-ups.
Low power endurance	• On routes or problems with more than thirty moves, you tend to get pumped, but you can do all the moves in ten- to fifteen-move sections. • You do well on short, continuous routes. • Power training may be your forte.
Limited recovery	• If you get a rest on route, you can't stay there longer than a minute without increasing your pump.

(continued)

Weakness	Signs & Symptoms (*continued*)
Low stamina	• You tend to be good for one or two good tries a day. • You can climb for only a few hours before tiring, even at your on-sight level. • You are done by the time everyone else has finished warming up.
Low power	• You fall off because you can't do the move rather than because you're too pumped. • You cannot climb very dynamically. • Friends seem to be able to do moves you cannot imagine.
Poor hip flexibility	• More-extreme leg and body movements can be impossible due to limited range. • You may experience lower-back pain. • You think the positions in the *Kama Sutra* are faked.
Poor focus	• You think about external conditions—pump, greasiness, heat, and so forth. • You have difficulty paying attention to the climbing. • You are easily distracted by background noise.
Poor memory	• You remember hand sequences, but not the foot sequence. • You rely heavily on tick marks. • You can remember the crux section of a route, but not all the moves or nuances of the route. • You have difficulty doing powerful cruxes on moderate routes, though you can do the moves.
Inability to control arousal	• You have difficulty maintaining a level of calm and focus on redpoint or on-sight tries.
Hasty decision-making	• You're better on-sighting or performing open skills. • You always know where you are going next.
Poor footwork	• Your foot skates off holds. • You tap your foot around finding the foothold. • You wear through a lot of rubber on your shoes. • You do not point with your toe onto the hold. • You stand on the small-toe area rather than closer to the big toe.
Inefficient technique	• You do not arch your back during movement. • You tend to have your legs fairly extended beneath you.

Weakness	Signs & Symptoms (*continued*)
Inefficient technique (*continued*)	• You need the extra muscle to hold the hold—this means you have poor grip strength.
	• You do not turn your chest away from the rock. You keep your chest front onto the rock.

Common Upper-limb Injuries	Associated Tendencies
Frequent finger injuries	• You tend to always crimp or always open-hand holds.
	• You don't stretch your forearms before, during, or after climbing.
	• You tend to climb with a front-on style and lock holds into your chest frequently.
Frequent elbow injuries	• You do not stretch your biceps and triceps muscles.
	• You have jiggly arm tissue behind the upper arm.
	• You cannot do a dip or a push-up.
Frequent shoulder injuries	• You have difficulty doing pull-ups.
	• You cannot use a high gaston.
	• You pull holds toward your body, bringing them close to your chest.

THE REDPOINT AND ON-SIGHT PRIORITY

If you have goals that are specifically related to either on-sighting or redpointing, then it is straightforward which elements are more of a priority than others. The harder the grade, the more important the elements of strength and power become. The more modest the grade, the better the mental skills, stamina, and technique need to be.

INDOOR PRIORITIES VERSUS OUTDOOR GOALS

Climbing movement outside is often very different from in the gym in a number of ways. While the gym can keep you fit for outside, it can also make outside climbing more challenging. The footholds aren't marked, and they usually don't protrude from the wall. Often you may also find that motions outside can be a little more challenging in that a route setter hasn't placed extra footholds and intermediates for short people. On the other hand, outside routes often have alternative sequences because there is more than just one way to do that section of climbing.

For many climbers, the transition from outside to inside climbing is relatively easy once you get over the change in atmosphere. Conversely, going from inside to outside is more difficult, both mentally and physically. To prepare yourself for outside climbing after a season indoors, the following exercises may be helpful. These are exercises that I have either made up or learned from other climbers along the way. You can use them to make the gym more interesting and challenging.

EXERCISE 1   ALL NATURAL

On the routes or boulder problems you make up, use only the natural features in the wall texture. This can be more difficult in some gyms than in others, depending on the texture. If your gym texture limits this activity, then attempt to substitute naturals on routes where they exist, but use taped feet where there are no naturals. Make sure you don't always select the perfect feet. Try to pick feet that will make you extend your leg out to the right, for example, when you need to go left. You could also incorporate a foothold that forces you to get more extended or more scrunched up than is comfortable.

EXERCISE 2   OPEN FEET

On climbing routes that are generally difficult for you, use any footholds, regardless of tape color. This may seem like cheating, and in many cases it will make the climbing easier, but it will also help you climb with the body positions that are more natural to you, rather than with style of the route setter. This exercise can help you make choices that bring you to the most efficient body positions.

EXERCISE 3   NATURALS & TRACKING

Climb routes and boulder problems using only the taped handholds or natural features in the texture for feet. This exercise can be particularly effective if used on boulder problems you learned that had open feet. It definitely increases the difficulty of the moves, but also helps you in bringing feet higher and sometimes using footholds farther away. This exercise is best done after you have become skilled at finding efficient body positions, allowing you to incorporate them and to be as efficient as possible on a powerful move.

THE PLATEAU DILEMMA
Continuously increasing the intensity of workouts is vital to seeing continued improvement in climbing performance. At some point, you may have experienced a feeling that you've been stuck at the same level of climbing for a long time. You may be asking yourself, What happened to those days of getting better on a weekly basis? This experience is called a plateau. Three things that can cause your performance to level off are undertraining, overtraining, and training the wrong thing.

Undertraining: Changing the Intensity
Many climbers reach a plateau in their performance because of continually climbing at the same intensity during each session of climbing. This is also called undertraining. By definition, training means working toward improvement, which involves challenging yourself and increasing the intensity of your sessions. Intensity can be heightened in three ways. First, increase the number of tries or moves in a climbing session, which works stamina. Second, decrease the rest time between attempts in a climbing session, allowing for enhanced recovery. Third, increase the difficulty of the moves, which builds strength.

Junior climber and client Robby O'Leary goes to the gym three to five times a week. He spends three to four hours there, sometimes on a rope and sometimes in the bouldering cave. Rob climbs with the Boulder Rock Club BlueWater Junior Climbing Team, and he has competed in all the local and regional competitions. In 1999 Robby qualified for the Junior Nationals and also the International competitions.

Prior to going to the International competition, he came to me for some advice and a training program. Given the nine weeks prior to the competition, I wrote a plan that increased the intensity of his recovery and power-endurance work in the initial seven weeks. This meant that from one week to the next, he had more to do with every gym climbing session. Some days, this meant decreasing the rest time between tries; other days, it meant doing more pitches at a higher difficulty. Not every session was an increase from the previous one.

The final two weeks, he tapered his training in order to have more rest prior to competing. Rob went to the Internationals and felt strong. He climbed well, placing fourth in his age division. He had placed fourth at the Nationals. Rob worked hard and continued to follow the plan, getting much better in the seven weeks he had available for training. But the real difference was that he increased the intensity of what he had been doing.

In any type of session, it is paramount that you change only one of these elements during the session, rather than all three at once. Changing all three at once exponentially increases the potential for injury. Deciding which to change depends on where you feel you need to work harder. Increasing the number of moves improves power-endurance and stamina elements, whereas increasing the difficulty improves more the power or high level of power-endurance aspect of climbing. Decreasing the rest time between tries forces working with fatigue and improving recovery. **Training involves improvement, not success or failure. The redpoints and the on-sights come, and at a quicker rate, with the improvement.**

Overtraining

Overtraining can have a negative effect, leading to a plateau, or, even worse, injury. The symptoms of overtraining are similar to those of a plateau. However, in addition, you may experience a lack of motivation, overall fatigue, and poor sleep quality. You may notice a change in your eating habits as well. It is important to note that you may be experiencing symptoms of overtraining and not realize it. If the problem has existed for quite a while, it can be difficult to know what the normal should feel like.

Climber Nick Sagar spent the entire winter of 1994–95 trying to climb a 5.13a in his local gym. With the arrival of spring, he made a trip to the wonders of Smith Rock, Oregon, and pitted himself against the slightly overhanging, sharp, and technical routes the area had to offer. His training paid off, and he successfully redpointed *Churning in the Wake* (5.13a), *Aggro Monkey* (5.13b), and *Rude Boys* (5.13b/c). Spurred on by this success, Nick continued to train and climb on his native ground in Canada. As August approached, he felt his desire calling him to Rifle, Colorado. Without a partner, but full of optimism, Nick set out for yet another four-week climbing trip. During this trip, he managed only one 5.13a and one 5.13a/b. No matter how much he climbed or rested or psyched himself up, he could not get another redpoint. Nick was suffering from overtraining. He returned to Canada, took a few weeks off, and by October was back in form and ready for his trip to the Red River Gorge in Kentucky.

If your plateau stems from overtraining, then rest is the obvious answer. But how much rest is enough? Every climber responds differently to training, and a large part of determining the rest you need is to determine the level of intensity at which you've been working. In Nick's case, he needed three weeks away from climbing. You may need only a week off, or you may need more than a few weeks. It really depends on how long you have been pushing yourself and on how hard you've been working. When she was climbing full-time, Mia Axon, one of the few women to have climbed 5.14 by 1996, would take four weeks around Christmastime and four weeks in the middle of the summer each year.

If you feel that is not necessary and would prefer other options, the most effective approach in training involves high-intensity sessions of a longer duration with maximum rest between sessions. If, for example, you train four days a week, then you want to train two days in a row, rest one day, then train two days and then rest two days. The training days after rest will be the most difficult movement days, either redpointing or power training. The second day on should result in lower performance levels and may be shorter in duration, but this will improve your ability to recover from higher-intensity days.

If you do shorter sessions, but more of them, with shorter rest periods in between, it is difficult to maximize your recovery. This can lead to a greater buildup in fatigue over a shorter period of time than if your sessions are of a higher intensity with more rest between them. It is not impossible to eventually train your body to respond to shorter sessions and less rest between them, but doing so may still affect your overall fatigue.

A key point to mention is that if you feel that two days of rest is too much and you climb better with less rest, it could be the affect of your warm-up rather than your recovery. In some cases, this appears to be the case because the body needs a longer warm-up period after an extended rest. If you try doing a few more routes to warm up, getting up to your project level a little more slowly, you may realize you can climb just as well after two days' rest, if not better. However there is always the trade-off of warming up to the extent of exhaustion and blowing your juice for the rest of the day.

Overtraining can also lead to burnout, which is discussed in greater detail in chapter 9. In some instances, the cause of burnout can be more mental than physical, although the effect may be the same. After climbing for many years and working as a route setter in Boulder, Colorado, Jim Redo had been experiencing numerous climbing-related injuries—first in the fingers, then in the elbows, then the biceps. With the first sign of pain, Jim would take a break from climbing. He would slowly attempt to come back to climbing, gradually getting on harder things and then increasing the number of pitches. Then—yikes—another twinge somewhere else. More time off. Jim is one of the best climbers for stretching and maintaining bodywork outside of just climbing. None of these tricks were working for him. Finally, he just took a longer period of time off. Months, in fact.

Jimmy came back getting psyched for a new season and for getting into shape. It was not to be. He again went through a cycle of twinges and rest. Finally, he talked to me about what was going on. The initial problem was overtraining and burnout. Jim spends many hours on a ladder screwing holds on a wall and then spends hours training. This overtraining led to the many injuries. He also began to suffer from burnout as a result of the discomfort and lack of progress in his climbing. With the decline in his motivation, Jim also experienced a decline in performance. For him, resting and stepping away from climbing was a good first step. The injuries were more deeply rooted than he realized, and he needed to do a little extra tissue work before he would be pain-free. Chapter 9 has more ideas on recovering from burnout.

Overtraining can have a negative effect on your performance and your motivation. Rest is the answer.

Training the Wrong Thing
We all fall victim to working our strengths, and this can also lead to limited improvement in our performance. If you feel that you fall into this category, the best thing to do is work on your weaknesses. For example, if you love to boulder and spend 80 percent of your time doing really hard moves, then get on a rope and do some laps. You may find it a demoralizing experience unless you can have fun with it, but there are benefits. You will enhance your body's ability to use oxygen and recover from a pump.

The body needs to work at different levels of intensity to improve overall performance. For example, runners will often do interval training or distance, even if the ultimate goal is the 400-meter sprint or the mile. During training, these runners will spend some practices running sprints, and other practices doing distance workouts. You can still improve without working at different difficulty levels; it just might take longer.

Climbing friend Mike Radicella experienced a plateau in performance that lasted for about a year. Mike took control of the problem by taking steps to improve while he continued to experience this leveling off. He did some personal coaching with my husband, Nick, and me. Mike's schedule with us forced him to structure his time in the gym a little more. A year later, he went out to one of his favorite climbing areas, Owens River Gorge, and did his most difficult redpoint to date. The ability to stay motivated without the reenforcement of improved performance was the key to Mike's success, along with his focus on working technical weaknesses and keeping it fun. Mike is a great partner because he just loves to climb regardless of the grade, the area, or his own personal success or failure. This positive attitude has helped him keep his motivation high, as well as the motivation of those he climbs with.

The Plateau Quiz

This quick quiz is designed to make you think about your current climbing performance. It will enable you to determine if you are experiencing a plateau—and if so, why. The previous section should help you know what to do about it. Circle T for true or F for false. The results are explained at the end of the quiz.

1. T F I climb at the same level I was one year ago.
2. T F I climb the same number of routes and routes of similar difficulty in a climbing session.
3. T F I usually climb four days a week or more.
4. T F I climb power endurance (that is, routes at my on-sight or red-point grade) 80 to100 percent of the time.
5. T F I almost always boulder.
6. T F I always (70 to100 percent of the time) do routes I feel comfortable climbing.

If you answered true to any of the above statements, you may be at a plateau or heading for one. If you answered true to statement 1, you have already reached a plateau. Statements 2 and 6 indicate that you undertrain, or climb only enough to maintain your current level of ability. Climbing four days a week or more could imply overtraining and a need to increase your rest or increase the intensity of a session as well as the rest between sessions. Statements 4 and 5 indicate a focus on one aspect of climbing more than others, which can limit the speed of improvement.

Identifying, acknowledging, and making changes are the three important steps to improving performance. Identifying a problem can be the most difficult part of the three-step process. Objectivity about your performance is essential to being able to identify problems. Carefully listening to others' feedback about your performance, monitoring your workouts or climbing days, and comparative analysis of the information can help you maintain objectivity. Keeping a journal recording your climbing performance—how many pitches, what grade, level of success or failure— gives you a resource to quantify what you can do and what you are doing. With this information, it becomes easier to know what changes will help you the most. Then you just have to make them.

Chapter 4

STRENGTH AND FLEXIBILITY WORK

*I*f physical weaknesses were demonstrated in the test results from chapter 2, the following exercises can be added to your climbing session to strengthen those particular elements of your foundation. *Do these exercises after you have completed climbing for the day.* If you do these exercises prior to climbing, you will be tired during your climbing session, and thus will have a lower chance of performing well and a greater chance of injuring yourself. Therefore, it is in your best interest to do these exercises just as you finish your climbing at the gym and have ten to twenty minutes before you leave. Remember that you will be doing these skills with fatigue, and so may not perform as well on these activities as you would when fresh. Despite your fatigue, it is important to think about form, not just success, when practicing these moves. The point is to increase strength and have a better foundation for climbing performance—not, for example, to excel at pull-ups.

GRIP-CONTACT STRENGTH

Different aspects of grip strength can be important to climbing. The first is contact strength, which involves being able to latch a hold. The second is a purer form of strength, which is the constant ability to use the hold as your body moves through a transition. In both cases, you are fighting the resistance of the hold under your hand—in other words, you are trying to prevent your hand from opening on the hold. In the first instance, you try to maintain the contact of the hold when you first latch it and your body's center of gravity is not underneath the hold. In the second instance, you are shifting your weight under the hold and possibly around the hold as you continue applying pressure to the hold.

In the first instance, it is difficult to maintain the hold because of the distance of the center of gravity from the hold and the limited contact with it. When you are hanging on one handhold and reach out to another, your hips are usually centered under the hold you reach from, or else they are moving with the body in the direction of the destination hold. There are situations where we can center our hips in such a way that they do not change position in the execution of the move, but eventually your hips must move as you adapt to positioning yourself under the next hold and set up to move to yet another hold.

The campus-board exercises are designed to assist you in training your contact strength, or in improving the ability to latch smaller holds that are farther away. To specifically train contact strength, try any of the campus exercises, bearing in mind that your goal is to use the smaller rungs. If you do not have the availability of a campus board, try to re-create the moves using similar holds on a section of wall that is slightly overhanging. When practicing these activities, remember to rest appropriately between tries. During each rest period, stretch the forearm extensors and flexors. These stretches are illustrated in chapter 10.

Grip-Resistance Work

In the second instance, it is difficult to maintain the hold because as your body moves around the hold, the wrist is changing orientation and increasing the length of the forearm muscle while it is contracting. This type of movement increases the strain on the tendon and pulleys, resulting in injury to one or the other. Although some people have recommended rolling weights through the hand as a training exercise for grip strength, it is ineffective if the wrist is not brought into the action. Similarly, just working contact strength, where the wrist is in a neutral position, does not improve your ability to maintain resistance on a hold when the wrist becomes extended. To accomplish this form of work, you have to lock off holds of progressively smaller sizes. Using the campus board as a tool, you can symmetrically work on this form of grip strength. All of the campus-board exercises, with the exceptions of the Contact Strength and the Doubles, will assist in this type of strength development. You may also incorporate the system-board moves that work lock-off strength. These exercises are found later in this chapter.

Back Strength

Back strength should not be confused with lock-off, or upper-arm strength. Back strength is illustrated in moves that require straight arms and large distances between holds. Moves involving a gaston out to the side and a measurable distance away work the upper back and the shoulder musculature. Another example would consist of getting to a hold that is out to the side and above the starting hold. In this example, you would not be able to keep the elbows bent, and your arms would be extended outward between the holds. Working this kind of action involves also working some core strength. Rather than revert to weighted pull-ups, try the system-board exercises that involve back strength and upper-body strength. Rather than tax yourself completely, you can execute these moves on moderate or big holds, unless you have limited time and wish to work grip strength as well.

Abdominal Strength

The type of strength required in climbing is not necessarily sit-up strength, or rather, the shortening of the abdominal muscles. Instead, it is the constant tension of the abdominal muscles while under resistance. Unfortunately, sport scientists have yet to discover a physical test for this strength that is easy to execute and consistent for different body sizes. Therefore, do not do sit-ups to improve your core strength. Rather, do the system-board exercises related to core strength and body tension at the end of this chapter, or try Pilates.

Hip Flexibility

Flexibility is discussed in greater detail toward the end of chapter 10. The important part to flexibility, in a climbing-related sense, is the need to have the opposing-muscle strength when attempting to gain the range of motion needed for the movement. This means that the strength in the quadriceps muscle must be adequate to lift the leg up high in front of the body, which in turn requires flexibility in the lower back and in the hamstring muscle. Similarly, it is beneficial for climbers to have strong adductor muscles and flexible abductors, as these are the muscles that assist in lifting the leg out to the side of the body.

Lower-Back Flexibility

Usually when lower-back flexibility is an issue, hip flexion may also be a problem. In your climbing, this may be reflected in your ability to perform high inside back steps or to step the foot through, between your leg and the wall. This action also requires a twist through the lower back at the same time the foot is placed high and close to the body. Use the hip-rotation exercises and the leg rotations to assist in increasing your range of motion. In addition, you can do the leg crossover stretch for middle-back flexibility. Again, the flexibility issues are discussed in greater detail in chapter 10, where you will find ideas on injury prevention, including examples of helpful stretches and muscle-strengthening activities related specifically to climbing.

CAMPUS-BOARD WORKOUTS

As an intermediate climber training in the climbing gym, I could monkey my way up and down the campus board. This success did not, however, translate into my climbing. Lock-off strength was not my problem. Contact strength was not a big issue for me, either. My weakness was that I could not always keep my feet on the footholds. Three years, many routes, and two number grades later, I could no longer do all the things I used to do on the campus board. My strength now is in my core, not in my back and upper arms. The campus board has now become a useful tool for me because it can isolate my weaknesses. After a few years of working on improving the efficiency of my movement, lock-off strength and contact strength have developed into weak links.

A campus board can be a useful tool in establishing greater grip-contact strength and lock-off strength. Core strength can also be developed with the use of the board. The following exercises are designed as a guide for you in using the board. The number of repetitions described may be well beneath your level or well above. Make the appropriate adjustments. If you cannot reach up two rungs, start by going up one rung. If you can easily go up one rung or two, use the hints to make the move harder or get on smaller rungs. You may also reach farther. If you find that you can easily do an exercise five times in a row for three sets, chances are that you do not need to continue to work on that particular exercise, or else you need to increase the difficulty.

Please note that many of these exercises have been described in other sources or are commonly practiced at various climbing gyms. This list is by no means complete, but rather, a small example of ways to work different muscle groups.

NOVICE/INTERMEDIATE LEVEL

Perform these tasks on smaller rungs to work more grip strength. Working on grip strength at the same time that you focus on back and shoulder strength is a healthy habit. Increased upper-arm strength relative to lower arm can create imbalances that can affect your climbing in two ways. First, you may adapt your style to cater to your strength. Second, you may increase your potential for injury.

CAMPUS BOARD 1	CONTACT STRENGTH

With both hands on rung 1 and with your feet on the lower foot bar, pull up as high as possible and hit rung 3 with your right hand. Lower yourself to rung 1, keeping your feet on the bar. Repeat, this time going up with your left hand. Continue this move for five hits with each hand. Try to increase the number of tries or sets of tries with subsequent sessions.

To make easier:

Go only to rung 2.

To make more difficult:

Take your feet off the back wall.

Try placing your feet on a higher rung.

Reach for a higher rung, rung 4.

CAMPUS BOARD 2   LOCK-OFF STRENGTH

Begin in the same starting position as in exercise 1. Pulling yourself as close to or past rung 1, hit as high as you can with your right hand. You may not latch a hold. That's OK. Just get as much height as possible. Repeat for the left side. Repeat on both sides for five tries.

To make easier:

Twist your body as you reach up with your hand.

To make more difficult:

Place only one foot on the back rung.

Place the opposite foot to the moving hand.

CAMPUS BOARD 3   LOCK-OFF TWIST

Starting with the left hand on rung 1 and the right hand on rung 2, the left foot on the low-foot rung and the right foot off. Pull in on the rungs and go to rung 4 with your left hand. Lower back to starting. Repeat this move five times, and then switch to work the opposite side.

To make easier:

Go to rung 3 instead of 4.

Put both feet on the back wall.

To make more difficult:

Take your foot off the back-foot rung.

Try going to rung 5.

Do not turn the body through the movement.

(continued)

CAMPUS BOARD 3   **LOCK-OFF TWIST (*continued*)**

ADVANCED MOVES

CAMPUS BOARD 4   **POWER THRUSTS**

Try starting on rung 1. Move one hand from rung 1 to rung 3. Then, without matching, move the other hand to rung 5. Then move the hand on 3 to 7 and the one on 5 to 9. Either climb down the board or jump off and repeat this exercise for five repetitions, and then return to it after sets of other movements or rest.

To make easier:

Walk your hands up the board, matching on each rung.

Start 1/2, go to 2/3, to 3/4, and so on.

Follow the pattern outlined.

Exception: match and then go again.

To make more difficult:

Increase the distance between your hands.

For example, start on 1 and 2, then go with hand from 1 to 4 and the hand on 2 to 5, and so on.

Extreme: try two hands on 2, go to 5 with one hand, then 8 with the other.

(continued)

CAMPUS BOARD 4 **POWER THRUSTS (*continued*)**

CAMPUS BOARD 5 **DOUBLES**

Starting with both hands on rung 2, feet off, pull yourself up to the rung and then throw your hands simultaneously to rung 3. This actually seems harder than it really is. Try it a few times to get a feel for the body movement involved. Continue up the board as far as is comfortable. You may jump down or lower down the board using a different movement unless you feel you are highly advanced at this activity (in which case, you probably don't need to be practicing it).

To make easier:
 Start on the biggest rungs you can find.

To make more difficult:
 Skip rung 3 and go to rung 4.
 Continue going up and down until you reach failure.

THE SYSTEM BOARD

A system board is an effective tool for improving your form in the execution of certain moves and in improving your strength. The intention is not always to get to the top of the board, but rather, to execute moves well. The following exercises work different elements of strength and body position. In trying these elements, ensure that you attempt movements in a static and controlled action. Bear in mind that you may have a very difficult or a relatively easy time with these moves depending on your personal strengths and weaknesses. If you find a particular activity extremely difficult or powerful, try to make it a little easier with the described actions. If the exercise is too easy, you can make it more difficult by reaching farther and holding the finish position, with your hand hovering for a count of five seconds.

These exercises have been compiled from sources including magazine articles and other climbers. You may have many other ideas—feel free to play with those concepts. Please use these practices as a guide to how to use the system board.

SYSTEM	**UNDERCLINGS**
BOARD 1	**works biceps and core**

Starting with your hands on the underclings, place your feet directly beneath the hold and move one hand up to the next hold of the underclings. Maintain body tension and bring the opposite hand to match. Repeat to failure or to the top of the board. If you have success, continue in sets. Remember to do the moves statically.

To make more difficult:

Place feet with a wider stance.

No matching—go directly to the next hold.

To make easier:

Turn with your body in the movement.

Bring feet to higher footholds.

SYSTEM	**HIGH STEP PULLS**
BOARD 2	**works upper arm, core, and lower back**

With your hands matched on holds of equal difficulty, step your left foot high directly under the handhold. Pull your upper body to the hold, then reach out and up with the right hand. Relax and repeat, switching feet and hands.

To make more difficult:

Try to lock the hold lower than shoulder height.

Pull in with only one hand.

Hover your hand as you reach.

Hold for a count of three to five seconds.

To make easier:

Place foot a little lower and out to the side a bit.

Move dynamically.

SYSTEM   **FOOT-EXTENDED LOCK-OFFS**
BOARD 3   **works lock-off strength, leg extensors, and core**

Hanging from holds of equal difficulty, place your right foot out to the right, with your leg almost fully extended, then flag the left foot. Pull your chest up to the hold in a front-on position at about 2 o'clock from the starting hold, reaching upward with the right hand. Repeat for the opposite side.

To make more difficult:

    Place the foot farther away.

    Pull with only one arm.

    Hover your hand as you reach.

    Hold for a count of three to five seconds.

To make easier:

    Bring the foot in closer to your body.

SYSTEM	WALK FEET DOWN
BOARD 4	**works core and foot strength**

Hanging on jugs, with your shoulders relaxed and arms straight, place your feet on holds and walk them down the footholds as far as you can. Hold the position for a count of five, then walk back up. Alternate which foot gets lower.

To make more difficult:

Hang on to smaller holds.

Work with feet farther apart.

Work with feet out to the side more.

To make easier:

Use bigger, more in-cut footholds.

Decrease the time you hold the position.

SYSTEM	FOOT GRABS
BOARD 5	**works foot strength and core tension**

Hanging with straight arms and relaxed shoulders, swing your feet into the wall and alternately grab footholds with your toes. The grab should be good enough to stop your swing. Release and repeat.

To make more difficult:

Start from a motionless position.

Reach with your leg out to a hold far enough away that it's hard to get. This works leg extension.

Try to get the footholds farther away.

To make easier:

Use large footholds (start higher on the board to be able to incorporate hand-holds as footholds for this exercise).

SYSTEM	INWARD-OPPOSITION DOUBLE THROWS
BOARD 6	**works core tension and contact strength**

Start with your hands pushing inward on the sides of the square holds. Place your feet directly beneath and throw your body upward, releasing both hands and latching the sides of the next row of holds. Maintain your feet on the holds. Once in control, bring your feet higher and repeat.

To make more difficult:

Keep feet lower.

Use smaller holds.

To make easier:

Throw with one hand, then the other.

SYSTEM BOARD 7	BODY ROLLS WITH OPPOSITE FOOT OUT TO SIDE works on obliques, leg extension, and upper-body strength

With your left hand on a jug and your right on a smaller and lower hold, place the right foot out and to the right, a little lower than your right hand. Using your whole body, roll your right shoulder up to the left hand and hold for a count of five seconds. Switch sides and repeat.

To make more difficult:
> Don't use your right hand in the movement.
> Place your foot farther from your hand.

To make easier:
> Bring the foot in closer to the body.
> Use jugs for both hands.

SYSTEM	DIAGONAL LOCK-OFFS
BOARD 8	**works obliques, back, and biceps**

With one hand on a hold, set your feet in a back step and flag. Stand up through the legs and reach as high as you can, trying to get to a like hold. Reset on a new hold, opposite hand and foot, and repeat.

To make more difficult:

Use smaller handholds.

To make easier:

Put the flagging foot on a foothold.

SYSTEM	**SHOULDER CROSSOVER**
BOARD 9	**works hip tension, back, and core**

Starting on a hold with your left hand, your right foot in a back-step position, and left foot opposing, reach right with the right hand, crossing the chest over the left arm. Once on the right handhold, pivot feet, reset foot positions, and repeat with left hand.

To make more difficult:

Use smaller handholds.

Flag the opposing foot.

To make easier:

Reach in a more upward direction.

SYSTEM
BOARD 10

FULL-BODY EXTENSION
works body tension

In a front-on style, work your hands up the system board, keeping the feet low. For example, move each hand up two holds, while your feet stay on the same holds. Move your feet up and repeat.

To make more difficult:

Use sloping footholds.

Make bigger hand movements upward.

To make easier:

Make smaller movements between holds.

Use big footholds.

TECHNIQUE TRAINING

Technique training is an extremely important part of improvement and involves many aspects, most discussed in chapter 8. If you don't do any technique training, then you should start. You can work on footwork during warm-ups, and you can practice body tension during power training or power-endurance training. Similarly, lock-off work can be done at the end of any session on a system board. If you need to make it fun, then I suggest finding a partner who is willing to work on it with you and make it into a game. For example, challenge each other to find the most efficient sequence on a boulder problem. Try the problem the way that feels most natural first, and then repeat the problem using a different style or sequence for the moves. This may mean that you eliminate footholds or handholds and basically create a new problem.

It is best to apply technique practice early in the climbing session, because as fatigue increases, your ability to properly apply technique decreases. The only exception to this rule is the system board. If you opt to work on a system board to work a particular technique, do your work after climbing. The system board will tire you, and you will not climb well during the session if the board is used early in the session.

Warming up is a great time to focus on particular techniques such as foot placement, shoulder rolls, and core-tension climbing. When warming down, you can also focus on breathing exercises and pace. These two elements require a little less focus than some other techniques. Select your technical weaknesses and focus on them one at a time during each warm-up route.

Chapter 5

WORKING
THE ELEMENTS

*A*ll athletes, from the serious to the recreational, benefit from a structured approach to practicing their skill—in other words, training. Runners don't just run the races; they do various distances, testing their power and their endurance. Dancers don't simply practice routines, but rather, they work on the individual technical skills that make up the routine as well as on the stamina to perform at a high skill level for more time than the program requires. Recreational athletes, however, just *do* their sport or activity. Likewise, most climbers just go and climb, and this can be a very satisfactory approach—no training, just doing.

Harder routes and more-challenging goals require a systematic approach for quick realization. If your sights are set on more-challenging routes or bigger numbers, you may be extending the time it takes to achieve these goals by not having a structured approach. Motivation, talent, and experience will take you only so far. There is also the element of training—not just your physical strengths and weaknesses, but your mental and technical skills as well.

Interestingly, various climbing destinations lend themselves to different physiological, mental, and technical strengths. Some of this could be due to the nature of the climbers who established the route, but some of it is due to the nature of the rock. For example, Smith Rock, Oregon, is known as the birthplace of sport climbing in North America. In an attempt to keep the routes mentally challenging, the bolts were spaced safely, but not comfortably, for most climbers pushing their limits at that grade. This leaves you in this area working on the mental challenges of climbing, trying to maintain your skin and crimp strength. On the other hand, the routes in Kentucky tend to have bolts spaced closer together. However, a pump develops from the constant open-handing of rounded sandstone, and your back musculature is dominating the majority of oxygen trying to get to your forearms.

If you visit Rifle, Colorado, the routes may strike you as being powerful between good rests. This requires a different mental and physiological focus than either Smith Rock or the Red River Gorge in Kentucky. Yet if you visit Red Rocks, just outside of Las Vegas, Nevada, you may think the climbing lends itself to more-continuously pumpy movement. Fortunately, you can prepare yourself for these things with a little training.

PHYSICAL TRAINING

Physical training is the easiest part to work on because weaknesses are most readily defined and thus targeted. If you don't have very good lock-off power, then you can set hard problems that force you to lock-off. If grip strength is an issue, and you're planning that trip to Smith Rock, you can climb on smaller holds, on a less-steep angle to force grip strength. The most important part of physical training is to mix up the elements that you work on. Bear in mind that you need to keep a solid foundation of strength, so focusing on weaknesses can give you this foundation by bringing all physical elements to the same level. **Tailoring a training program to fit you requires an understanding of your strengths and weaknesses, your motivation and goals.**

Most climbers go to the gym or the crag and climb a few-warm up routes, then move on to the more challenging routes, things they try to redpoint or on-sight. They get pumped and they go home. This is the routine, and slowly they progress from one route to another, eventually making the step through the grades. For some, this progression is slow and steady; for others, it comes to a standstill. On the other hand, there are numerous bouldering enthusiasts who avoid tying into a rope at all costs. Put them on a problem that goes up for more than 15 feet, and they fall off repeatedly. The problem is called a plateau. The way to fix this is to change the climbing program.

If you spend all of your climbing time focused on one element of climbing—for example, power endurance at a redpoint or on-sight level as described in the previous paragraph—you may do very well at that one element, but even in that physiological arena, your progress may be slower than you would like. Power is great, but without an improvement in recovery or power endurance, you limit the number of moves, and therefore the amount of technique you practice, and the continual improvement in your VO_2 max. **Generally speaking, including all the elements of climbing in a training program or climbing schedule is essential to a successful program.**

FOCUSING ON THE ELEMENTS

The remainder of this chapter deals with ways to work the different elements outlined in chapter 1. For ease of understanding, examples of climbers of different levels of ability training these elements have been described. If you apply these examples to your own climbing, tailor them to fit you. For example, the amount of rest to take between routes or attempts is only a guide. If you find your performance is continually diminished to the point that you don't feel like you can get anything done, increase the rest between tries by five to ten minutes.

THE KEYS TO TRAINING

The tricks to training are by no means secret. Many authors have described the following concepts. In the event that you haven't seen them before or need a reminder, here they are again.

1. Constantly push the limits of the element you are training. If you succeed on all your tries and rest enough to maintain high performance levels, you are not re-

ally training at your limit. In the examples described below, the point is to be failing most of the time, because by failing, you can see weaknesses more clearly and learn what needs to be changed to improve your performance. The rest times are limited to allow you to get more accomplished, and the idea is to get really fatigued. This means to increase the intensity of your physical work through a series of climbing sessions. There are three ways to raise the intensity. First, try harder routes or problems, working on strength. Second, increase the number of moves either by doing more pitches or longer sets of climbing time, enhancing your stamina. Third, decrease the time you rest, as illustrated in the example. Reduced rest improves your recovery.

A very important injury-prevention tip is to raise the intensity by changing only one factor at a time. If you try to increase your work in all areas at once, you are at a greater risk for injury. Similarly, if this is a new concept to you, try progressing relatively slowly at first, increasing the workload only once every three or four climbing days. If you climb only once a week, you could try raising the intensity every other or every third climbing day.

2. Work on all the physiological aspects of climbing—endurance, stamina, recovery, power endurance, and power. Mixing things up provides a diversity that can keep you interested. Incorporate more climbers into your experiences, allowing you to learn from other people and develop needed elements faster. Power can be improved at a faster rate when time is spent specifically focused on that aspect of climbing. Similarly, the capillaries supplying the muscles with oxygen are developed faster with endurance training than with power-endurance training.

3. Spend more time on the things you always fail with, and develop this part of your foundation. Psychologically, failing becomes easier to live with when it happens more often, and you learn to measure gains in smaller steps. Working on a weakness such as climbing on steep terrain can open up the options of routes you can try and have success in doing.

4. Climbing should be fun—that's why you do it. If the pleasure is derived from success, then your goals need to be designed to allow you to feel the success. If the best part is just experience, then allow many climbing days of just experience and enjoyment. Work on climbing only when you feel OK with its being work. The secret to motivation is keeping it fun!

TRAINING POWER

Power training involves working at a high difficulty level doing five to eight moves. Power is about increasing your ability to recruit a higher percentage of muscle fibers for one explosive contraction. Therefore, the movements are more difficult, involving longer pulls, lower lock-offs, steeper angles, and smaller holds. The best way to determine power problems is to look for routes that are harder than your current redpoint level. After giving yourself a little time to figure out how to do the moves, determine if they are eventually doable. If so, keep trying. If you just cannot figure out the moves, then it may be less power training and more frustrating, so look for another problem. A sample plan for power looks like the following in exercise 4.

EXERCISE 4	POWER TRAINING

For this example, you redpoint 5.10-mid and on-sight 5.9. You have a good balance of power relative to power endurance.

Warm-up:
 5.9 boulder problem three times with two minutes' rest between each try.

Activity:
Problem A (V2):
 First try: start to hold 3 (failure); rest two minutes.
 Second try: start to hold 3 (failure); rest two minutes.
 Third try: figured move 2/3 to 4 (failure); rest two minutes.
 Fourth try: start to hold 4 (failure); rest two minutes.
 Fifth try: start to hold 6 (failure); rest two minutes.
 Sixth try: start to hold 3 (failure); rest fifteen minutes.
Problem B (V2):
 Six tries (similar to above example).
 Repeat for problems C through E, all being V1 or V2.
 Last problem: one try of each of problems A through E.

Warm-down:
 Light and moderate movement on 5.6 or 5.7 moves.
 Note: If you do not understand the V scale, see the appendix.

EXERCISE 5	FOUR-BY-FOURS

This is one of my favorite activities, especially given my love of high-intensity movement and my lack of power endurance. I do not know its origin, but highly appreciate the fun. Depending on how frequently you fall during this exercise, it can be considered power or a very high intensity of power-endurance climbing. This example applies to a 5.13– redpoint climber, hence the power limit should be higher than 5.13–.

Warm-up:
 5.11– short problem (twenty-four moves); rest eight to ten minutes.
 5.12+ short problem (fifteen moves); rest ten to twelve minutes.
 5.13– short problem (eight to twelve moves); rest twelve minutes.

Activity:
 5.13+ (two to four moves); 5.13+ (two to five moves); 5.13-mid (two to six moves); 5.13– (five to seven moves); rest fifteen minutes.
 Note: It should be difficult to complete all the problems, but try to do all four.
 If doing a power-endurance session, the grades would be 5.12+ (six to nine moves); 5.13– (four to seven moves); 5.13– (four to eight moves); 5.12+ (six to nine moves). Repeat this pattern for three to five tries. Allow fifteen to twenty minutes' rest between each session.

Warm-down:
 5.11+ or ten easy boulder problems of twenty moves.
 Note: You can alter this activity by decreasing the rest time between the sets of four problems. This will push your recovery.

TRAINING POWER ENDURANCE

Power endurance can be trained in numerous ways and at different levels of difficulty. The activities are outlined according to high level or a low level of power endurance. For redpoint climbing, look at the high-level exercises. For power endurance in more than eighty moves, look under the low-level category.

High Level of Power Endurance

To train for redpoints, power-endurance training involves routes at the redpoint level or above and increasing the pump by climbing with fatigue. This exercise can also be considered a recovery activity. Training can begin on a route once you know the sequence. The following are examples of redpoint training days for a climber redpointing 5.12–.

EXERCISE 6   RECOVERY ON ROUTES & LAPPING ROUTES

Warm-up:

    5.9; rest fifteen to twenty minutes.

    5.10– or -mid; rest fifteen to twenty minutes.

    5.10+ or 5.11–; rest fifteen to twenty minutes.

Activity:

    When feeling warmed up: 5.12–; climb to failure, then lower to an easier section and get back on quickly after the fall (stay at this rest section to diminish pump if necessary). Continue through the rest of the route, completing overlapping sections of the route.

    Rest fifteen to twenty minutes.

    Repeat this on the same route or on one of similar difficulty, until you begin to have trouble getting to your high point and doing the route in three or four sections.

Warm-down:

    After a rest of twenty minutes, 5.10–.

    Rest twenty minutes, then climb a 5.9 or 5.8, making sure that you are not getting pumped during the warm-down.

EXERCISE 7 | **CLIMBING FROM THE TOP DOWN**

For this example, the climber redpoints 5.11a.

Warm-up:

  5.8; rest fifteen to twenty minutes.

  5.9; rest fifteen to twenty minutes.

  5.10-mid; rest fifteen to twenty minutes.

Activity:

  5.11– or 5.10+; climb until failure, then get back on the route and climb to the top. Rest fifteen to twenty minutes. Repeat the same route, climbing to point of failure. Lower to a few moves below the place you fell on the first try. Attempt to climb through to the top of the route. Rest fifteen to twenty minutes.

  Repeat process until you are not getting through sections normally easy for you. Rest fifteen to twenty minutes.

Warm-down:

  Do a 5.9 and a 5.8.

  This is a common redpoint strategy of climbing a route from the top down. The benefit is to be able to add to your pump by adding more and more moves to the route. This approach works best for climbers who are falling because of the pump as opposed to a powerful crux in the route.

EXERCISE 8 | **POWER-ENDURANCE LAP AND A HALF**

Also effective to training for redpoint climbing is lapping the route. In this situation, you climb the route, quickly getting back on after a fall, and continue to the top. From the top, you lower to the ground and start the route again without rest, thus increasing the number of moves at this level of difficulty and the pump. Again remember to follow a similar warm-up and warm-down pattern as described in exercises 3 and 4.

  To improve a very high intensity of power endurance, which can occur after powerful cruxes with limited rest and continuous climbing, select a boulder problem that you recently redpointed and can usually redpoint now. Do the problem, then come down and move directly (no rest) to another problem of similar difficulty. Continue this activity, putting together as many problems as possible. The limit should be around four in a row. If not, you may have to select more-difficult problems.

Low Level of Power Endurance

Power endurance can also be improved by working at the on-sight level by also increasing the number of moves. In this case, you stop when you fall the first time, which is usually around the second or third lap. This type of work improves more of the endurance aspect of power-endurance physiology, a more important element for on-sighting than power or high-intensity (difficulty) power endurance. The example used for the description of exercise 9 is designed for a 5.10– on-sight climber. Adjust the difficulty accordingly for your level of ability.

EXERCISE 9	LAPPING ROUTES

Warm-up:

   5.8; rest twenty minutes.

   5.9; rest twenty minutes.

   5.9; rest fifteen to twenty minutes.

Activity:

   5.10a previously done, then go to anchors, lower to ground, repeat, lower again, and repeat until failure. (This should be on the third lap; if not, the grade or route is too easy.)

   Rest twenty minutes. Repeat above exercise on harder route.

   Rest twenty to twenty-five minutes. Repeat above exercise a third time.

   Rest twenty minutes. Warm down on two routes (5.9 and 5.8).

   Adjust the difficulty of the routes according to your own redpoint and on-sight levels.

RECOVERY TRAINING

Recovery requires a different approach, involving climbing with fatigue and minimizing rest time. Recovery is important at various levels of difficulty—for example, being able to continue power-endurance climbing after a powerful crux section with limited rest, or climbing routes with ongoing power endurance from start to finish.

   To improve recovery on routes with continuous climbing of a certain intensity, you can do something at the redpoint level, lowering to the ground and getting right back on, going as far as possible. Instead of doing the thirty moves of the route, you now have done forty-five moves of continuous climbing. This is also suggested for training power endurance at a high level of difficulty.

   Power-endurance recovery can be improved by doing a route at the redpoint level, climbing to a point of pump, and moving into a rest and staying on these holds until the pump diminishes or until a minimum time—for example, four minutes—has passed. If not in the gym, this activity can be done by lowering to a rest section of the route or by hanging on the rope. However, hanging on the rope is not quite as effective as hanging on some holds and trying to recover. A sample session incorporating this type of work is described in exercise 10.

EXERCISE 10   GETTING IN THE REST

Assume that your redpoint level is at the 5.11-mid range and that you on-sight 5.10.
Warm-up:
> 5.9; rest fifteen to twenty minutes.
> 5.10–; rest fifteen to twenty minutes.
> 5.10+; rest fifteen to twenty minutes.

Activity:
> 5.11-mid; climb halfway or until pumped, then move onto big holds and find a resting position. Stay in this position, switching hands and recovering from the pump for a minimum of three minutes. Continue on the route, repeating this resting exercise as necessary. Rest fifteen to twenty minutes. Repeat the above exercise on same route or other routes until too fatigued to get recovery in rest positions. Note: To improve recovery on small holds, pick a route a little easier (5.10+) and go half way. Get on moderate to small holds, stay for two minutes, and then continue to the anchors.

Warm-down:
> 5.9; rest twenty minutes; repeat.

EXERCISE 11   INTERVAL TRAINING

Finally, you can improve recovery by doing what are known as intervals. This encompasses doing a hard route, an easy route, a hard route, and an easy route—with no rest between each try. This gets you pumped on the hard route and gives time on the easy route to flush out the pump.

Assume that you redpoint at the 5.9 level and on-sight 5.8 on a good day.
Warm-up:
> 5.6; rest fifteen to twenty minutes.
> 5.7; rest fifteen to twenty minutes.
> 5.8; rest fifteen to twenty minutes.

Activity:
> 5.8 (well known); 5.7 or 6; 5.8 (again well known); 5.6; rest twenty minutes. Repeat for three to four sets or until continuously falling on the first or third route.

Warm-down:
> 5.6 twice with a twenty-minute rest between tries.

You can adapt this activity with a heart-rate monitor. Begin by knowing your maximum heart rate (max HR) prior to beginning this activity. Climb the 5.8, then check your heart rate, noting it and determining how close it is to 80 or 85 percent of your max HR. Move quickly to the 5.6 or 5.7 and try to decrease your heart rate to a level closer to your resting heart rate, but still within 65 percent of your maximum heart rate. To calculate your maximum heart rate, use the following equation. (This equation came with the Freestyle heart-rate monitor I purchased. There are many other equations out there—if you have one that you prefer, use it.)

(continued)

EXERCISE 11   **INTERVAL TRAINING** *(continued)*

210 – (half your age) – (0.05 × weight) + 4 = max HR for men

Example: for a 30-year-old male weighing 160 pounds
max HR = 210 – 15 – 8 + 4 = 191

max HR × 0.5 = 65% of max HR   191 × 0.65 = 124
max HR × 0.8 = 80% of max HR   191 × 0.85 = 162

Using this example, you would want to be close to 162 beats per minute after climbing the 5.8, and then lower your rate to approximately 124 beats per minute while
on the 5.6 or 5.7. If your heart rate is higher than the 80 to 85 percent values on the
5.8, then try easier routes. If the heart rate remains closer to the 50 percent or less
value on the 5.8, then try harder routes.

STAMINA TRAINING

EXERCISE 12   **GETTING MORE DONE**

Increasing stamina involves climbing more routes than you normally attempt to do.
To successfully accomplish this may mean dropping back the difficulty of the routes—
or at least of some of the routes—and increasing rest time between routes. For example, if you normally climb six routes a day, none harder than 5.11–, then you may do
only one route at the 5.11 level and seven or eight routes between 5.8 and 5.10. This
will certainly take more time, and the last few routes should be somewhat difficult to
complete regardless of the grade. Repetition of these types of climbing days will eventually make it easier to be able to do eight or nine routes in a day.

The opportunity to go on a road trip is appealing to most climbers. There is a
chance to work outside, to do numerous pitches, and to climb a number of days in
a row. Unfortunately, most climbers haven't developed a good enough base to do
this and stay injury-free. For some, it is a reoccurrence of a chronic problem; for others, it's a new acute injury. The best way to get in shape for a long weekend of
climbing is to start by getting into the gym a few days in a row. Again, decrease the
difficulty of the routes you are trying and increase the rest between tries. Try to do
as many routes as you normally do, and don't forget to warm down really well.

TRAINING ENDURANCE

EXERCISE 13   **ENDURANCE**

Endurance takes the most time to train because the intensity is so low and the volume of work has to be high to reap the benefits. During endurance climbing, there is no pump. For most experienced climbers, it involves continuous movement for twenty to thirty minutes or more, although beginners may not be able to work endurance immediately. Just as in aerobics—because this is aerobic climbing—you want to increase your heart rate to 80 percent of maximum and keep it there for twenty minutes. Finding a belayer who is willing to hang in this long can be difficult. Doing an easy, long, multipitch route can be the solution. Having to think about the protection and just enjoying the experience of being high off the ground can keep you going for twenty minutes of continuous climbing. If stuck in the gym while working on endurance, using your own personal music player can help if you are not always excited by the gym's selection of music. You can also improve this activity by making a game out of it if you have a partner or two to work with. For example, transporting carabiners from one area of the wall to another and back again before you can stop can help keep you going.

WARMING DOWN AND RESTING

Most people suffer from the effects of postclimbing fatigue because they haven't warmed down effectively. An effective warm-down includes doing routes well below your ability. For example, if you on-sight 5.10–, then do 5.6 or 5.7. If you don't have time for more routes, then try very low resistance on a rowing machine. At the very least, sit in a hot bath after a climbing session and do twenty to thirty minutes of stretching before you go to bed.

The Austrian National Ski Team dominated in the Super G during the 1998–99 season. The team coaches attribute this success to better warm-downs. The team members skied some warm-up runs, followed by approximately six fast and difficult runs. The warm-down consisted of getting on a bike and spinning, with low resistance, for about twenty minutes. After this, a blood sample was taken and assessed for the level of lactic acid. Each team member had to continue on the bike until all traces of fatigue were eliminated from the blood. The theory behind this is that diminished levels of lactic acid in the muscle, along with increased oxygenation of the muscle, followed by healthy eating to replete the nutrient loss through exercise, equal better recovery at a faster pace.

Exercise physiologist and former weight lifter Mike Caldwell expressed concerns with this form of practice, citing the importance of lactic acid in the promotion of muscle growth and as a gauge for recovery. The stiffness and soreness of muscle tissue tells you that you are not fully recovered, and that you need to rest until the discomfort dissipates. This muscle messaging is the way the body informs you that you are prepared to go back to physical work.

So who's right? In a sense, both schools of thought are correct. Warming down can enhance the immediate rate of recovery by decreasing the oxygen debt created during the activity. Likewise, there are numerous microtears and trauma to the muscle during an intense workout. It is important to be aware of the signals the body uses to warn you of injury potential. However, most of us don't have personal technicians to complete this same postclimbing test. And most of us are not trying to win World Cups. This means that we do not tax our bodies to the same extent that world-class athletes do. Nonetheless, you can get on some really easy routes— or use a rowing machine and go with low resistance—to promote the warming-down effects. Muscle stiffness is a natural reminder to take it easy—if you ignore this warning sign, you risk injury. It is important to continue warming down for five minutes longer than you think you need to. **Warming down effectively can greatly enhance recovery.**

NUTRITION
Eat properly before and after climbing sessions—lots of protein if you've been working on the strength issues, more carbohydrates if you focused on stamina and endurance work. Eating during a day of climbing should consist of easily digestible foods that aren't too high in sugar. Unlike the endurance sports, you have time where you sit around and belay. Food high in carbohydrates or sugar can just make you sleepy or give you a quick high that peters out between pitches. A little protein and fat throughout the day can assist in keeping your energy level up without the shakes you get from caffeine. Caffeine may perk you up, but it can also dehydrate you and increase your potential for injury. So remember to drink lots of water. More about nutrition is discussed in chapter 10.

ON-SIGHTING VERSUS REDPOINTING
Within the population of climbers, there are some who will excel at redpointing routes, whereas others tend to excel at on-sighting routes. There are debates over which is a more notable ascent of a route. In traditional climbing, climbers would just complete the route and not go back to rehearse it until the route could be ac-complished without falling. Redpointing was initially found to be very distasteful to many climbers, who believed such ascents less distinguished.

On-sighting requires the climber to recognize patterns of movement prior to physical knowledge of a route, defined by sport scientists as a means of determin-ing expertise. In addition, the climber must also execute the moves and maintain an optimum level of anxiety to perform the task without falling. This type of skill can be compared to basketball, where the player must quickly identify the play that needs to be executed to successfully score in a rapidly developing environment. Sport experts call this type of skill an open skill.

In such sports as figure skating or gymnastics, the programs are well rehearsed before execution in front of an audience. In this form of sport performance, the abil-ity to maintain an optimum level of anxiety and execute very challenging skills is similar to the required tasks in redpointing. Because the environment is not rapidly changing for the redpoint climber, and because there is knowledge of the terrain, this type of skill is considered a closed skill.

Open and closed skills require quite different talents. In open skills, the ability to rapidly take in, interpret, and respond are of the utmost importance to success. These are more cognitive-oriented skills. Sports such as basketball and hockey are great illustrations of the application of open skills. The athletes are constantly taking in information about the placement of players and the movement of the ball or puck. They then must respond quickly to an ever-changing situation.

In a redpoint situation on routes or bouldering, or in the execution of closed skills, the climber deals with a greater physical demand from the body and must use highly tuned kinesthetic awareness to realize success. A mistake in the nuance of movement can mean falling on the route. In figure skating or gymnastics, the competitors are executing a series of closed skills while following a routine.

As with many sports, the implementation of closed skills demands a great deal of focus on the progress of the movement. This means that the environment remains very predictable, or, as some would term it, monotonous. For some people, this becomes very tiring, and they have difficulty continuing to work in this manner. A great example of this is seen in running, which demands a continued repetitive motion. A focus on the repetition is boring and makes you want to stop. Avid runner and good friend Mike Radicella says that "if you start thinking about stopping, you will." However, if you keep thinking about your pace or the route you plan to run, you can continue much farther. The closed skill requires this ability to focus on nuances of the necessary movements and process, as well as the effort needed to carry them out. If the thoughts are interrupted or if you are distracted from the moves, you are likely to fall, especially if the route is truly at your limit.

DEVELOPING OPEN AND CLOSED SKILLS
Being better at quickly processing information requires attention to understanding body positions, given a selection of hand- and footholds, the ability to tune out unnecessary information, and the ability to execute the movements. Listed below are sample exercises to enhance performance of open skills.

EXERCISE 14   **OPEN SKILL 1**

Select a route, three or four grades below current on-sight level. Using a pencil and piece of paper, draw the route and describe the body positions used to execute moves during the on-sight. For example, left hand on sloper, right foot dropknee, left foot directly below sloper to move to right-hand crimp. Attempt to describe all the body positions.

Note: To make this task easier, sequence the hands first, then go back and sequence the feet, using the same hand sequence. On the third time sequencing the route, visualize the body position. You can check yourself by having a partner videotape your ascent. Compare your notes with the actual videotaped performance. The closer your expected sequence is to the actual sequence used, the better you are with this skill.

Variation:

If a camera is not readily available, you can also do this exercise by describing your plan—that is, the body positions—to a climbing partner. Have that individual watch your ascent and give you feedback on how accurate your proposed plan was to the actual ascent.

EXERCISE 15	OPEN SKILL 2

Using a selection of five holds—three handholds and two footholds—describe or visualize three ways to complete a move with the same hand, from the two starting handholds to the next hold. You must find three ways prior to trying the moves. After you have determined three movement patterns, decide which will be the most efficient, not necessarily the most effective. Try each and observe whether all three were possible and whether you correctly identified the most efficient as opposed to the most effective.

Note: The definitions of efficient verses effective are found in the glossary.

EXERCISE 16	CLOSED SKILL 1

In this exercise, use the list below to find three things about the movement. Then repeat the movement three times, trying to keep those three elements the same with each attempt.

Nuances to notice:
1. amount of pressure applied on the handholds
2. position of the hips during movement
3. pressure through the toe
4. pull in the leg as the hips shift
5. tightness in the upper back during movement
6. rotation in the wrist during transition between holds

Once the movement can be executed with the three elements in mind, progress to a problem that requires a more difficult transition—one that you have a 50 percent chance of doing—and repeat the exercise.

Variation:
Increase the number of nuances you focus on during the movement. This will tax your ability to process information while executing the movement. However, make the progression reasonable.

EXERCISE 17	CLOSED SKILL 2

While climbing on a boulder problem or route at the redpoint limit, or what would ideally be the redpoint limit, focus only on the movement. Block out all information and noise from other sources. Repeat in your mind the sequence of moves as you continue through each series of moves. For some people, it helps to repeat verbal messages in their head while attempting to ignore other distractions. To make this easier, try more-difficult problems and continuously difficult moves. Eventually work into applying this skill while in a rest position on a route.

MENTAL TRAINING
Mental training is the part of climbing I dislike the most, and it is therefore the least motivating climbing I do. Some people love the mental challenges climbing has to offer. Either way, we all can use a little training in this arena, as we do in the techni-

cal and physical form as well. Chapter 9 deals with activities geared to improving mental climbing performance in detail. However, with all these other elements, where does mental practice come into the picture? Mental training can be practiced during every climbing session on warm-ups or while doing harder routes at the on-sight or redpoint level. It can provide you with a great sense of empowerment, and can therefore be truly rewarding if you allow it to be.

As with any training practice, too much focus can lead to decreased motivation. If you begin to dread climbing because you hate taking the lead falls or despise rehearsing every route prior to climbing it, then cut back on the amount of time you focus on mental training. For some people, it works better to practice on just the first three routes of the day, while others would rather practice continuously through the day, but only every third climbing day. Although you may dislike the prospects of challenging your fear, facing it is the best way to overcome it. You will have to eventually feel uncomfortable in order to process and deal with your fears in climbing.

These principles apply to technique work as well. Trying to move in new ways can be just as difficult and uncomfortable as running it out 5 feet more than we usually do. However, you do not have to jump 40 feet to get over your fear and discomfort. Take the process in stride, increasing the stakes a little at a time if that works best for you. Find what works for you by allowing climbing to be fun, yet making sure that you are progressing in the mental arena also.

Note that training open and closed skills is also a part of mental training. Other elements such as confidence and focus are also important aspects of mental training and are covered in greater detail in chapter 9.

Mental training is as important as physical and technical training. The trick to better mental performance is to step outside your comfort zone and push your mental stamina.

Chapter 6

BIG GOALS AND
SO LITTLE TIME

*B*ecause many of you have numerous responsibilities in your lives, climbing is something that, as much as you love it, gets put fairly low on your list of things to do. This does not mean that you can't continue to do more and more challenging routes. It does not have to mean that you must train. What is especially important is that you enjoy your precious climbing time. Use this section of the book to help you use your time to your advantage and get all you want out of climbing.

MAKING THE TIME FOR CLIMBING
The biggest difficulty for many people pulled by a lot of strings—including a partner, children, or career—is setting aside the time for climbing. Although climbing is a form of recreation—something you do for fun and a little physical activity—it can also improve your productivity and clarity within other aspects of your life. Research shows that a certain level of physical exertion or adrenaline rush can improve the mental processes of the brain. Furthermore, the empowerment gained in climbing can enhance self-esteem. These are important elements in personal development and great excuses to make time for climbing.

All interested climbers will make the same initial steps. These include devising goals, determining the priority of climbing in the scope of all things in life, and outlining the plan of attacking weaknesses and maintaining strengths. Climbers who have little time for climbing in relation to other priorities in their lives have a few options in focusing their approach to climbing time and structuring that time. For those who climb as much as possible, though limited by time and fortune, read into the next chapter and see if you can afford the compromises required. Or perhaps a combination of plans would work better for you.

SETTING GOALS
One of the best ways to determine what you like and dislike about something is to set goals. As previously mentioned, there are different types of goals. Performance goals describe success or failure at something. Progress goals, or objectives, are the steps we take to achieve our performance goals. Objectives are the more general statements that lead to success in performance goals, and they are very measurable.

Performance goals must be specific, including a time frame, a specific route or grade, and a level of success that is measurable. For example, you may start with the idea that you want to be more consistent on 5.9. From there, you must determine what consistent means. Does it mean redpointing 50 percent of the 5.9's you try? Does it mean on-sighting 75 percent of all the 5.9's you try? The second step is to set a time frame in which you need to accomplish this goal. We would all like to be climbing harder tomorrow, but the time reference needs to be realistic. If you are not sure of what is realistic, then think about how many days you actually climb in a week or a month. Try to determine how many days of work it will take to improve to this level. (This is difficult initially but becomes easier with practice.) You can establish more than one goal for a given time frame, and you can determine performance goals related to physical, technical, or mental weakness. Now you know that your goal really means you want to on-sight 50 percent of all the 5.9's you try by the end of three months. This goal is measurable—you will either be able to do this or you won't.

Performance goals and progress goals must be measurable. If you say that you want to be able to improve footwork, you have stated a goal that has various interpretations. Does it mean being better at foot placement, or does it mean being quieter with your feet? Or does it mean you want to be able to select the correct foot more quickly? Perhaps it means you want to be quick at stepping the right part of your shoe on the hold. Maybe it means all of these things. Without a clear definition, you might believe that the goal can be achieved more readily than is possible. This can limit progress.

The best way to accomplish your goals is to select goals that encompass your love for the sport. You may have to set progress goals to guide you to achieving your performance goals, but the big goal is in the arena most enjoyable to you. For example, some climbers love to on-sight routes, considering it the purest form of climbing. Without doing routes with harder moves—that is, redpoints or boulder problems—this climber will have more difficulty improving his or her on-sight performance. Without doing harder moves, it becomes troublesome to on-sight those moves. Whereas a majority of time may be spent focused on on-sight skills, some time must also be spent on learning to do powerful moves of a greater difficulty, improved technique, and a high level of power endurance.

With this in mind, go to the end of the chapter and write your performance goals—one set to be accomplished within the next three months, another in a six months time frame, and a third in twelve months. Remember to make these goals measurable and specific. After you write your goals, ask yourself if you can put a yes-or-no answer by that goal, given a specific date. If you can, it is a quantifiable goal, which is what you need.

For each of the performance goals listed, write three progress goals you will need to accomplish in order to know that you stand a good chance of achieving the performance goal. For example, a performance goal to redpoint a V3 boulder problem would require the ability to do V3 moves, to do V2 boulder problems, and to do V0 problems quickly, perhaps within four or five tries. To determine your progress goals, consider your weaknesses and what level of fitness and strength you will need for the performance goal. Use the examples below to assist you in determining your performance and progress goals. You may find it beneficial to start a journal with a record of your goals, current weaknesses and strengths, and an outline for a future plan, which you should have by the end of the chapter. A journal can be a helpful tool. Use it to keep track of your progress and (if you can find time) your climbing sessions. The information you record allows you to see how different activities and focus can work for you—or perhaps not work for you.

SAMPLE 1

Performance goal:
1. to redpoint 5.12a
2. to on-sight 5.11a
3. to boulder V5

Progress goals:
1. a) to do two tries on 5.12a, resting five minutes between tries and with a total of only four falls
   b) to redpoint three 5.11c's
   c) to redpoint two 5.11d's
2. a) to on-sight one 5.10+
   b) to do two and a half laps on 5.10+
   c) to do three laps on 5.10b
3. a) to do a V3 boulder problem of fourteen moves
   b) to increase grip-strength-to-weight ratio to 0.75, and back-and-shoulder-strength-to-weight ratio to 1.80
   c) to do V5 moves or all the moves on a 5.12+

These goals outline the physical skills that are required to reach the performance goals. You may incorporate mental or technical climbing goals as well. For example, it would also be crucial to be able to lead at that level with a strict focus on the climbing.

SAMPLE 2

Mental goals:
To lead a 5.11d, taking one fall when totally pumped.
To take three warm-up falls. Plan when and where on the route to take them, and make sure to take them.
To lead on a route to two moves past what is comfortable before saying take. This has to be done at least twice on each lead and on at least four routes per day.

SAMPLE 3

Technique goals:

To watch your feet as they are placed and weighted on footholds for the first two warm-ups.

To make up four boulder problems requiring dropknees and to successfully complete the problems. The difficulty should be such that they cannot be done in the first day of trying.

To do three sets of five attempts at diagonals on the system board. (Diagonals are described in chapter 4.)

THE BASIC APPROACH

The shortest step you can take to improving your climbing performance is to increase the intensity over time. This can be done regardless of how much or how little you climb. It takes only remembering how many pitches and the grade you regularly do, and then adding to that. Most people go climbing and, due to time restrictions or the social component of climbing, climb only the same difficulty of routes or the same number. This is akin to running the same distance in the same time. You will not get faster or run farther until you push yourself a little harder.

Increasing the intensity involves doing more-difficult moves to develop strength, or increasing the number of moves within the session overall, thus building your stamina. The third way to increase intensity involves decreasing your rest during the session. This forces you to climb with more fatigue, thus refining your recovery. The important thing to keep in mind is that too much at once can lead to injury. Therefore, it is best to pay close attention to how your body responds to this change. Rest when you need to. Never increase all three factors of intensity at the same time. It would be ideal to set a goal to increase the intensity every three or four climbing sessions, depending on your fitness level and the amount you get to climb. Everyone has different rates of recovery, and everyone's body responds differently to fatigue. This means that you need to be attentive to the messages from your body in deciding when and how to increase the intensity.

Contrary to this, my friend and sometime climbing partner Matt O'Connor loves to repeat the same circuit of problems over and over. Despite a busy schedule at the Boulder Rock Club—and the responsibility of keeping up with his wife, who is a far better athlete than many of us can hope to be—Matt finds time to hide out in his garage and work on the circuit of boulder problems he has designed on a structure just a hair taller than Matt himself. Using this confined space to work on problems that he has devised, Matt can be entertained for hours. He can never do the problems the first time, but with continual work, Matt manages to eventually succeed. Then he adds a few new problems. He always goes back to his problems and does them again on another climbing day. Sometimes Matt will try to link two problems together once he can successfully do them individually. The key to his continued improvement is that Matt keeps raising the level of difficulty. By using his older problems as a measuring stick of his recovery, he is able to determine when to increase the intensity.

MANAGING THESE ELEMENTS
The Interval Plan

For those with a limited time for climbing, there are two practical approaches that will change your climbing and prevent a plateau. The first is interval training. This includes working on the different elements of power, power endurance, recovery, and endurance (and/or stamina) continuously over a period of weeks. The big plus to an interval cycle is that it allows for more flexibility and is widely practiced in sports that require attention to different technical elements and skills, as with dance or gymnastics or basketball. Technique training can be done in every session regardless of the physiological element being practiced. Thus, with interval training, you can work on straight-arm body positions while doing hard boulder problems or while working on stamina.

Interval training allows you to compensate for short training sessions, without trying to find more time later. This flexibility also allows you to vary the people you climb with, by working on different things while with some partners, but not with others, who may be more inflexible in their plan. An outline of the program is seen in figure 1.

FIGURE 1			INTERVAL PLAN			
Sun.	**Mon.**	**Tues.**	**Wed.**	**Thurs.**	**Fri.**	**Sat.**
E or S	Rest	Rest	P or PE	PE	Rest	PE/R

E = endurance   P = power   R = recovery
S = stamina   PE = power endurance

Refer to chapter 5 for specific exercises for working these elements.

Pros and Cons of the Interval Plan

This approach has advantages and disadvantages, which you will find in the lists below. Weigh the pros against the cons to decide whether this practice approach is right for you. There are no right or wrong answers, only your own answers. You may find you don't have time for a plan at all. That's OK, too.

The basic concept with the interval plan is to mix up your approaches to climbing. In other words, sometimes do routes, but at other times, do harder moves on boulder problems. Or you may opt to do laps at a lower level of difficulty, but decrease your rest while you put all those extra moves together. This can be done with an increase in intensity over the course of numerous climbing days. With time, you will see better performance. Just remember that the more structured you are, the faster you will see augmented performance.

Pros:
- You want flexibility in time during the day for training elements.
- You can focus more on other weaknesses, rather than most specifically on physiological training (mental tricks).
- You prefer diversity.
- You prefer to see continuous progress.
- Interval work requires a long training session only every *x* number of days, rather than many long days in a row, as with other plans.
- This plan can be designed around climbing days, giving you flexibility in how many days a week you climb.

Cons:
- You probably won't see a peak at end of the cycle.
- If you are traveling to different climbing areas, it is harder to practice.
- The less you climb, the longer it will take to see progress.
- There are more factors affecting performance in a session, so it can be difficult to compare one session to another.
- Because this plan is less disciplined, it can be easier to fall into old habits.

With this list of priorities, now sort through the most important elements in the lists of pros and cons. It is important to be honest with yourself rather than trying to do things that are not really what you prefer to do. And don't let what you think you "should" do interfere with what you can do.

Focused Interval Plan
The second training program involves a combination of the above-mentioned plan and a periodized plan. This combination is referred to as a focused interval plan. More specifically, you may mix up the elements throughout a week of climbing, but you may spend a higher percentage of time working on one element than the others. This type of program also allows for a great deal of flexibility, though not as much as a simple interval plan.

A focused interval plan is designed to meet your individual weaknesses. Specifically, if power is one of your weaknesses, this plan allows you to focus attention on power, but still gives you flexibility to continue to work on your stamina, power endurance, recovery, and endurance. There is a greater emphasis placed on the power training until your level of power is on a par with the other elements. This plan outlines a continued shift among the elements of power, power endurance, stamina, and recovery, with a greater focus on improving power endurance at a lower level.

This example plan is designed for those who have a disparity between their onsight level and their redpoint level, or those who cannot recover on routes that are five or six grades below the redpoint level. The introductory focus is on working on routes around the on-sight grade or a little harder, but not quite as hard as the maximum redpoint level. After a few weeks, with a better foundation and more equality between strengths, the plan shifts to an equal focus on all four elements. This continues for the following five weeks, like the interval plan described above. The end of the cycle allows for some added rest and then, if things have been planned well, a spike in overall performance related to the specific goals for the climber. The plan would look different if the climber wanted to improve his or her power performance, for example.

FIGURE 2		**FOCUSED INTERVAL PLAN 1**	
Week	**Element Focus**		**Additional Days**
1	low power endurance, 2 days a week		power & recovery, 1 day each
2	low power endurance, 2 days a week		high power endurance & stamina, 1 day each
3 & 4	repeat weeks 1 & 2		repeat weeks 1 & 2
5	recovery & high power endurance, 1 day a week		low & high power endurance, 1 day each
6	recovery & high power endurance, 1 day a week		stamina & power, 1 day each
7 to 12	repeat weeks 5 & 6		repeat weeks 5 & 6
13	power endurance, power, stamina, 1 day each		decrease intensity
14	repeat week 13	PEAK	climb with normal intensity
15 to 18	rest		no climbing

Pros and Cons of the Focused Interval Plan

This plan also has benefits and drawbacks for different personalities and schedules. If you have a particular weakness, this plan can be designed to incorporate a higher focus on your weakness, improving it and your overall performance. The difficulty with this type of plan is that it requires a greater level of discipline. As with the interval cycle, prioritize the pros and cons listed below to determine how appropriate this type of plan is for you.

Pros:
- There is flexibility in which day you train certain elements.
- You can focus more on weakness, rather than on physiological training.
- This plan is more effective if traveling to areas that cater to specific training.
- For some, the diversity of this plan is more motivational than other plans.
- You can see continuous progress from one session to the next.
- Interval work requires only a long training session every *x* number of days, rather than many long days in a row, as with other plans.
- This plan can be designed around climbing days, giving you flexibility in the number of days a week you climb.

Cons:
- This plan doesn't lend itself to as high a peak at the end of a cycle.
- There are factors that can affect performance, making it difficult to gauge improvement.
- This plan requires some discipline on your part in order to be successful.
- The less you climb, the longer it will take to see progress.
- If you neglect the plan for a week or two, it is difficult to pick up where you left off.

CONSTRUCTING THE PLAN

You now should understand what the elements are (power, power endurance, stamina, endurance, and recovery), how to train them (specific activities to work each element), and how to put together a plan—either an interval plan or a focused interval plan. This is part of the equation to improving your performance. The next step is understanding what specifically you need to work on and the priority of attention. For example, you may know that you need to greatly improve your recovery, you know to incorporate more recovery climbing sessions in the plan you've chosen (a focused interval plan, for example), and you know that you need to work on core-tension climbing. To develop the day-by-day plan, complete the following steps:

1. In order of priority, list your areas of weakness.

2. List the number of days per week you want, and reasonably can expect, to climb. If possible, note which days you plan to climb.

3. Outline the time of your sessions—for example: Monday night, two hours; Saturday, six hours.

4. Specify the type of program you want to try, either interval or a focused interval plan.

5. Determine the number of weeks you want to work on this cycle. The most effective time for a cycle would be between nine and twenty-four weeks. For initial training cycles, smaller cycles would reduce the chance for injury and give you the opportunity to see how the cycle works for you.

With this list and the list of goals, outline the weeks of the cycle on a calendar or a sheet of paper (see form 3, below). In the first week, write out the types of climbing sessions you plan to have. Describe how many routes, at what grade, and the number of tries. You can use your current intensity for the first week. In the second week, increase the intensity of each session in one of the three ways described previously. That is, increase the number of moves or tries, or decrease the rest (except in power sessions), or increase the difficulty of the moves. Continue in this pattern until you have successfully described each week in succession. Remember to continually gauge your success at completing the required work for each session. If it becomes too hard to accomplish, either physically or mentally, you will quit. It's okay to stop increasing the intensity for a few weeks if necessary. Try to implement games, or else climb with people who motivate you or are excited for you to successfully accomplish all that you set out to do in a given climbing session. This is the best recipe for success.

FORM 2   **CLIMBING GOALS**

Performance Goals:

   1.

   2.

   3.

Progress Goals or Objectives:

   1. a)

       b)

       c)

   2. a)

       b)

       c)

   3. a)

       b)

       c)

FORM 3   **YOUR PLAN**

TYPE OF CYCLE

Interval Plan   Focused Interval Plan   Increase Intensity

NUMBER OF WEEKS

PRIORITY OF WEAKNESSES

Endurance   Power Endurance   Power   Stamina   Recovery en route

Grip strength   Back strength   Core strength   Upper-arm strength

Closed skills   Open skills   Footwork   Straight arms   Hip shifts

DAYS PER WEEK OF CLIMBING

FORM 4	THE PLAN
Week number	**Activity Plan for Each Climbing Session**
WEEK 1	
WEEK 2	
WEEK 3	
WEEK 4	
WEEK 5	
WEEK 6	
WEEK 7	
WEEK 8	
WEEK 9	
WEEK 10	
WEEK 11	
WEEK 12	

Note: It is very important that you go into a power-training day with at least twenty-four hours' rest, and that you rest at least twelve hours after the session. If you have a high level of recovery, you can minimize your rest. If you have a lower level of recovery, it is better to rest more, thus decreasing your chances for injury.

Chapter 7

MORE TIME AND BIGGER GOALS

*I*f your goals are to become the best climber you can be, to be in the winner's circle, and/or to do the hardest routes, your approach to training will have to be more intense and limited. To be at the top of the field requires dedication to some aspects of climbing you may prefer to ignore. It also requires sacrificing what you may want to do for what you should do. However, if a really focused plan makes climbing a chore, change the plan. If you stop climbing, you will never get better.

You can still get better using either plan outlined in chapter 6, and you will improve faster if you have more time to commit. The more flexible approach, however, better suits a climber who feels stifled under a highly structured plan.

SETTING GOALS

If you've had trouble deciding which idea to focus on, start with this first step. Set some goals. As previously mentioned, there are different types of goals. Performance goals describe success or failure at something. Progress goals are the steps or objectives we plan to accomplish in the pursuit of our performance goals.

Performance goals must be specific, including a time frame, a specific route or grade, and a level of success that is measurable. For example, you may start with a concept such as wanting to redpoint 5.13b by August 1 of this year. The key to a performance goal is a specific performance at a specified time. You either have done it or haven't by a certain date. If this step seems difficult, move on to the second step and think about how many days you actually climb in a week or a month. Then try to determine how many days of work it will take to improve to this level. If a 13b redpoint level is your aspiration, and you currently climb only 5.12+, then recognize how long it took you to get from 12c to 12d. To get from 12d to 13a will take probably at least that long, and then that time again to reach a 13b redpoint. Take into account things that may interfere with this plan—weather, chronic injuries, and so forth.

You may also want to establish more than one goal for a given time frame, allowing you to improve performance in a couple of areas rather than just one. These other goals may be related to on-sight performance, technical-skill improvement, power, or mental weaknesses. Working on power and on-sight skill will help you become a better redpoint climber by preventing plateaus in performance, and by increasing stamina and the ability to do hard moves.

The best way to ensure that your ability will come close to accomplishing your goals is to select goals that encompass your love for the sport. Bear in mind, however, that striving for top-five placing in a World Cup will mean that you cannot always do only what you love to do in climbing. You may get the most enjoyment out of climbing outside, but training for competitions is going to focus a great deal of your attention on gym climbing. You may have to set progress goals to guide you in achieving your performance goals, but the big goal should encompass the climber's love for the sport. You may appreciate the movement aspect of climbing more than any other element and want to be able to do hard redpoints. While power training will help you improve your ability to do hard moves, recovery and stamina will also be necessary to enhance your overall power endurance at the redpoint level.

With this in mind, go to the end of the chapter and write three performance goals. The first goal should be accomplished within the next three months, the second should target a six-month period, and the third should be completed by the end of twelve months.

For each of the performance goals listed, write three progress goals you will need to accomplish in order to stand a good chance of achieving the performance goal. To determine your progress goals, consider your weaknesses and what level of fitness and strength you will need for the performance goal. Use the examples below to assist you in determining your performance and progress goals.

SAMPLE 4

Performance goals:
  1. to redpoint 5.13d
  2. to on-sight 5.13a
  3. to boulder V10
Progress goals:
  1. a) to do two tries on 5.13d, no rest between tries,
       and with a total of only four falls
      b) to redpoint three 5.13b's
      c) to redpoint two 5.13c's
  2. a) to on-sight one 5.12+
      b) to do two and a half laps on 5.12c
      c) to do three laps on 5.12b
  3. a) to do a V8 boulder problem of fourteen moves
      b) to do two hours of stretching a week
      c) to do V10 moves

These goals outline the physical needs that are required to reach the performance goals, although you may incorporate mental or technical climbing goals as well.

SAMPLE 5

Mental goals:
To compete in one National competition and two regional competitions during the year.
To compete in at least four local competitions.
To maintain a heart rate below 80 percent of maximum prior to climbing a route in a competition.

SAMPLE 6

Technique goals:
To watch feet as they are placed and weighted on footholds for first two warm-ups.
To make up four boulder problems requiring one high-footed move and to successfully complete the problems. The problems should be of the V8 or V9 difficulty.
To do three sets of five attempts at diagonals on the system board, using slopers spaced 30 inches apart.
This should provide you with several ideas for progress goals and how to determine them.

MANAGING THESE ELEMENTS
Periodized Training
There are three potential ways to change your climbing and see a shift from a plateau. The first is periodized training, which involves spending weeks working on one element—for example, endurance—then shifting into a power-endurance phase, and finally, a few weeks later, doing power training. Dale Goddard and Udo Neumann describe periodized training in their book *Performance Rock Climbing*. Figure 3, below, gives an overview of what periodized training looks like. This sets up the climber for a peak in his or her performance over the course of a few weeks. There are pros and cons to this training regime, and it doesn't suit all climbers.

FIGURE 3	**PERIODIZED PLAN**			
Endurance (stamina)	Power endurance	Power	Peak	Rest
weeks 1–6	5–12	11–14	15	16–18

This plan involves following one element for a period of weeks, then moving to another for a number of weeks, and finally doing a third element. After working on each element, all have improved, and you anticipate a peak in performance. Using the above plan, during week 14, you would decrease your intensity in your climbing days. This would boost your rest and allow for a peak in your performance during week 15. All of this is assuming that you have trained appropriately through weeks 1 to 14.

Pros and Cons of Periodized Training

Periodized training has benefits and drawbacks for different personalities and schedules. If you have a particular weakness, this plan can be designed to incorporate a higher focus on your weakness, improving it and your overall performance. The difficulty of this type of plan is that it requires a very high level of commitment.

Pros:

- This plan is very disciplined, a benefit for those who like structure.
- You can see continued improvement as you increase the intensity.
- If you time things right, there is a peak period.
- This plan targets weaknesses well.
- This works well if in a particular climbing area (for example, *The Happy and Sad Boulders* in Bishop, Ca.) when training power.

Cons:

- With less diversity, it can be hard to stay motivated.
- Periodization requires large time blocks for endurance climbing over the first number of weeks.
- You may not like the inflexibility of the plan.
- If you misjudge your training or your rest, it may mean that you won't see a peak in your performance.

Interval Training

A second option for training includes working on the different elements of power, power endurance, recovery, and endurance (or stamina), each in their own cycle. Interval training, as this is known, allows for a little more flexibility and is widely practiced in sports that require attention to different technical elements—for example, figure skating. If you have difficulty allowing for weeks of endurance training every day, this plan provides opportunity to avoid this, still seeing improvement. An outline of the program is seen in figure 4.

FIGURE 4			INTERVAL PLAN			
Sun.	Mon.	Tues.	Wed.	Thurs.	Fri.	Sat.
E or S	Rest	Rest	P or PE	PE	Rest	PE/R

E = endurance   P = power   R = recovery
S = stamina   PE = power endurance

Refer to chapter 5 for specific exercises for working these elements.

Pros and Cons of the Interval Plan

This approach has advantages and disadvantages, which you will find in the lists below. Weigh the pros against the cons to decide whether this practice approach is right for you.

Pros:

- Time flexibility for training elements.
- You can focus more on other weaknesses, rather than most specifically on physiological training.
- For some, this plan is more motivational because of its diversity.

- You can see continuous progress.
- Interval work requires only a long training session every x number of days, rather than many long days in a row, as with other plans.
- This plan can be designed around climbing days, giving you flexibility in how many days a week you climb.

Cons:

- You probably won't see a peak at the end of the cycle.
- If you are traveling to different climbing areas, it is harder to practice.
- The less you climb, the longer it will take to see progress.
- There are more factors affecting performance in a session, so it can be difficult to compare one session to another.
- Because this plan is less disciplined, it can be easier to fall into having no plan at all.

Focused Interval Plan

The third potential training program involves a combination of the above-mentioned plan and a periodized plan. More specifically, you may mix up the elements throughout a week of climbing, but you may spend a higher percentage of time working on one element than the others. This type of program also allows for a great deal of flexibility, though perhaps not as much as a plain interval plan.

A focused interval plan is designed to meet your specific weakness—for example, power—while allowing you to continue to improve your stamina, power endurance, and recovery. There is a greater emphasis placed on the power training until your level of power is on par with the other elements. This particular plan focuses on improving an overall foundation in the first four weeks, and then shifting to a more power-oriented program through the remainder of the cycle. The example in figure 5 focuses on improved power endurance at a level around the onsight difficulty.

FIGURE 5	FOCUSED INTERVAL PLAN 2	
Week	Element Focus	Additional Days
1	recovery & stamina, 1 day a week	power & high power endurance, 1 day each
2	recovery & power, 1 day a week	high power endurance & stamina, 1 day each
3 & 4	repeat weeks 1 & 2	repeat weeks 1 & 2
5	power & high power endurance, 1 day a week	low power endurance & recovery, 1 day each
6	power, 2 days a week	stamina, 1 day a week
7–12	repeat weeks 5 & 6	repeat weeks 5 & 6
13	power endurance & power, 2 days each	decrease intensity
14	repeat week 13 PEAK	climb with normal intensity
15 to 18	REST	NO CLIMBING

Pros and Cons of the Focused Interval Plan

This plan also has benefits and drawbacks for different personalities and schedules. If you have a particular weakness, this plan can be designed to incorporate a higher focus on your weakness, improving it and your overall performance. The difficulty of this type of plan is that it requires a greater level of discipline. As with the interval cycle, prioritize the pros and cons listed below to determine if this type of plan is right for you.

Pros:

- There is flexibility in which day you train certain elements.
- You can focus more on other weaknesses, rather than on physiological training.
- This plan is more effective if traveling to areas that cater to specific training.
- For some, the diversity of this plan is more motivational than other plans.
- You can see continuous progress from week to week.
- Interval work requires only a long training session every x number of days, rather than many long days in a row, as with other plans.
- This plan can be designed around climbing days, giving you flexibility in how many days a week you climb.

Cons:

- This plan doesn't lend itself to as high a peak at the end of a cycle.
- There are factors that can affect performance, making it difficult to gauge improvement.
- This plan requires some discipline on your part in order to be successful.
- The less you climb, the longer it will take to see progress.
- If you neglect the plan for a week or two, it is difficult to pick up where you left off.

CONSTRUCTING THE PLAN

You now should understand what the elements are (power, power endurance, stamina, endurance, and recovery), how to train them (specific activities to work each element), and how to put together a plan—be it a periodized plan, an interval plan, or a focused interval plan. You should also understand that the first step to take in improving your performance is shifting your focus from one element to incorporating all the elements. The second step is to increase the intensity of work you do in a climbing session. If you combine this with understanding what specifically you need to work on, and the priority of attention, you will more readily see performance gains. For example, you may know that you need to greatly improve your recovery, you know that you need to incorporate more recovery days in the plan that you've chosen (a focused interval plan, for example), and you know that you need to work on core-tension climbing. To develop the day-by-day plan, complete the following steps:

1. In order of priority, list your areas of weakness.

2. Write down the number of days per week you want, and reasonably can expect, to climb.

3. Outline the time of your sessions—for example: Tuesday night, four hours; Wednesday night, four hours; Saturday, eight hours; and Sunday, eight hours.

4. Specify the type of program you want to try, either periodized, interval, or a combination.

5. Determine the number of weeks you want to work on this cycle. The most effective time for a cycle would be between nine weeks and twenty-four weeks. For initial training cycles, smaller cycles would reduce the chance for injury and lessen the time commitment of a plan that works for you.

With this list and the list of goals, outline the weeks of the cycle on a calendar or a sheet of paper. In the first week, write out the number and types of climbing sessions you plan to have. Describe how many routes, at what grade, and the number of tries. You can use your current intensity for the first week. In the second week, increase the intensity of each session in one of the three ways described previously. That is, increase the number of moves or tries, or decrease the rest, or increase the difficulty of the moves.

BEYOND NORMAL FITNESS

For some of us, getting to the level of climbing 5.12 or 5.13 is enough. For others, climbing 5.8 is inspirational and fulfilling. However, there are those climbers who want to be the best, who want to push their bodies beyond the hardest routes out there. These climbers are fewer in number; for them, the rules above don't seem to apply. Kids are another example where the above rules seem not to apply. But they do. The people who can redpoint 5.14 after six previous attempts, or who can climb three and four days in a row, have conditioned themselves to do this. You can condition yourself to do this, too.

For climbers such as Chris Sharma—who climbs 5.14 at the end of the day, second day on—you know that 5.14 isn't his limit. Chris has conditioned himself to climb that well by working on routes that are harder than that, and by failing numerous times late in the day or on his second climbing day. Likewise, top North American climber Tommy Caldwell has done some of his best routes late in the day after numerous attempts. Most of us have to send (redpoint) within the first three tries, or that's it for the day. But most of us, unlike Tommy, appreciate resting. The deep, dark secret Tommy holds in his heart is that he would never have to rest.

Conditioning is not the only reason climbers such as Tommy Caldwell, Dave Graham, or Chris Sharma can excel—there is much to be said about their motivation and the way they mentally approach routes or problems. The less chance for success, the harder they try. For most of us, the more tired we are, the more we are apt to let go. Really good climbers can push their mental and physical elements well beyond what feels comfortable.

Tommy is just as human as the rest of us, however. Nick Sagar and Tommy spent a few weeks outside of Newcastle, Colorado, working on a trail to a new cliff in the Clinetop Range. The hike in was a continuous uphill approach. Tommy approached this route—which consists of 5.14b climbing for 50 feet to another 5.14b section—with a minimal shake between the two sections. (Nick described the "rest" as nothing more than an opportunity to chalk.) After a number of days hiking into the *Fortress of Solitude,* working on his project named *Kryptonite,* Tommy approached this day like the others. A little rest, and he would try again. Tommy, however, fell asleep with his head resting on a pop can. Not many of us can say we push ourselves this hard during a day out at the cliff or in the gym.

GETTING TO THIS POINT

If you are dedicated to climbing and want to push the limits, training and being outside what is comfortable is what it takes. Nick Sagar believes that what makes some of the best climbers excel is their ability to continue to push themselves when the mental and physical intensity of the route is extremely high. For most of us, the feeling of being so outside of our comfort zone is overwhelming—as a result, we stop climbing. The difference is, the best don't stop. They continue until absolute physical failure, and then they try again.

Nick related to me his experience of watching the Bindhammer brothers demonstrate this prowess. These two brothers are very strong European competitive climbers. One evening in France, they arrived at the cliff, warmed up on an 8a+ (5.13c) on-sight. Then they proceeded to something more challenging, 8c (5.14b). Late in the day as the sun was setting, one of the brothers tried a 7c+ (5.13a) on-sight. He climbed up and clearly got his hands crossed up in the crux on the smallest holds of the route. He tried to change his feet, tried to release one hand, then the other. Each potential change indicated that to continue would mean a fall. The brother reverted to his original crossed-up position. He stayed there. He continued to stay in this position, unable to climb through, for two to three minutes, until he began to shake and eventually fail on the handholds. He would not let go. Regardless of how hopeless the situation seemed, he continued until absolute physical failure.

Most of us do not do this, and most of us do not on-sight 7c+ (5.13a) like the Bindhammers do. **This type of tenacity demands that you listen very carefully to the messages from your body. You will be walking a very fine line between injury and progress. You must become a prudent judge of every ache and pain when you hear the tremor through your body. Remember that it is always better to err on the side of rest than to sustain even a minor injury.**

IMPROVED CONDITIONING

Training to climb more than four days a week at a redpoint level, or three days a week at a power level, requires better conditioning. However, there is a more prudent way to approach it that can decrease some of the potential for injury. The following is a guideline for conditioning yourself to climb more days a week at a high level of intensity.

In this example, you climb four days a week, generally in a pattern of two climbing days, one day of rest, followed by two more climbing days and two days of rest. Then you repeat this cycle. At the point where you decide you are going to try to incorporate more climbing days, you are getting in six-hour sessions and working at your redpoint level of 5.13d for three and a half hours of the six-hour session. You also work on 5.13d routes during your second day of climbing, and generally can do five or six tries at this level on both the first and second day. You tend to experience a decline in performance after the third try on a route; on a good day, after the fourth try.

Plans for Increasing Climbing Fitness

Initial plan

Day 1	Day 2	Day 3	Day 4	Day 5	Day 6
6 hours (5.13d)	6 hours (5.13d)	rest day	6 hours (5.13d)	6 hours (5.13d)	rest day
Day 7	start on day 1 and repeat cycle				
rest					

To increase the number of climbing days in a week, you first need to improve your recovery between climbing days. The first step will be to decrease the intensity of the climbing sessions so you won't be as tired at the end of the day. The second thing to do will be to figure out a new pattern of climbing days. There are two approaches to this. The first would be to climb three days in a row, take a day off, then climb two days in a row and rest two days. This actually equals eight days, but over a pattern of four weeks, you will have increased your climbing days to eighteen, from sixteen out of twenty-eight days.

Modified plan #1 for increasing climbing days

Day 1	Day 2	Day 3	Day 4	Day 5	Day 6
5 hours (5.13d)	4 hours (5.13c)	rest day	4 hours (5.13c)	4 hours (5.13b)	5 hours (5.13a)
Day 7	Day 8	start on day 1 and repeat cycle			
rest	rest				

The second approach would be to organize your days so you eliminate a rest day. For example, you could climb two days on with one day off, two days on, one day off, and then two days on followed by two rest days. This structure again gives you eighteen climbing days out of a twenty-eight-day cycle. The benefit to this type of plan is in the structure of rest between the climbing days. More rest means you have an increased opportunity for success over climbing on a third day. The choice, however, depends on you. While you may respond better to one form of climbing organization, someone else may see better results with a different pattern.

Modified plan #2 for increasing climbing days

Day 1	Day 2	Day 3	Day 4	Day 5	Day 6
5 hours (5.13d)	4 hours (5.13d)	rest	5 hours (5.13c)	4 hours (5.13c)	rest

Day 7	Day 8	Day 9	Day 10	start on day 1 and repeat cycle
5 hours (5.13c)	4 hours (5.13c)	rest	rest	

In either case, you will need to decrease the intensity of the climbing days initially. If you want to be able to do powerful sequences on the fifth climbing day, then you don't want to decrease the level of difficulty. You may want to either increase the rest time between the tries you do in the day, or else limit the number of redpoint tries. So rather than waiting thirty minutes between your burns at 5.13d, you want to wait forty-five, or as much as sixty, minutes between tries. This could be the strategy for the first day climbing after a rest day. On the second day in a row of climbing, decrease the overall number of tries from six to four. With this pattern in place for two or three weeks, you can then begin to decrease the rest time, or increase the difficulty to trying a few 5.14a routes a day, or increase the number of tries you give on 5.13d. Eventually you should be able to be back to six tries a day at your redpoint level. Once at this point, you want to continue to increase the intensity in each session.

During the time when you are increasing the number of days you train, you should not expect to be redpointing at your limit. You can still be trying, but success should be limited. The amount of fatigue that your body is dealing with should be higher than what it is used to, which means that you should be climbing with more fatigue than normal. Once you have adapted to the increase in climbing days, or if you take an extra day off early in this new pattern, you may see better performance.

Increasing your climbing if you are in a periodized plan and training power can also be accomplished, but with caution. Suppose you are doing three power days per week—climbing day on, day off, with two rest days after three power-climbing days—and want to increase it. The first step would be to decide how, either doing two power days in a row or taking only two days off after four power-training days. Again, you would decrease the number of tries per session AND increase the rest time during the session. In the interest of preventing injury, it would be best initially to change both elements for at least the first cycle, then gradually work back up to your regular intensity after two or three cycles.

This principle can be applied to an interval training plan as well. If you are on an interval plan and you climb four days a week, you might do one power day, followed by a stamina day. After one rest day, you do a redpointing day, followed by a recovery day and then two days of rest. Again, you have the options mentioned above of climbing three days in a row with one rest day, followed by two climbing days and two rest days. Or the second choice would be to do two days in a row with one rest day, repeat that twice, and add one more rest day. Refer to the following diagrams for further explanation.

Original climbing plan

Day 1	Day 2	Day 3	Day 4	Day 5	Day 6
power	stamina	rest	power endurance	recovery	rest

Day 7	Day 8
rest	repeat from day 1

Modified plan #1 to increase climbing days

Day 1	Day 2	Day 3	Day 4	Day 5	Day 6
power	stamina	endurance	rest	power endurance	recovery

Day 7	Day 8	Day 9
rest	rest	repeat from day 1

This option follows the first example of climbing three days in a row. Note that this means a very-low-intensity climbing day, though with time, the intensity may be increased.

Modified plan #2 to increase climbing days

Day 1	Day 2	Day 3	Day 4	Day 5	Day 6
power	stamina	rest	power endurance	recovery	rest

Day 7	Day 8	Day 9	Day 10	Day 11
high power endurance	on-sight	rest	rest	repeat from day 1

This method of increasing time allows for more rest between climbing days, and thus a bit more recovery. Note that performance may not be optimal initially on days 7 and 8.

Opting to do three climbing days in a row would require that you decrease the intensity of the days, again by decreasing the number of tries or by increasing your rest time between tries. On the third climbing day, you would also want to be climbing routes of a lower grade, so you may start by adding a stamina day or a day of climbing intervals, only below the on-sight level. After a rest day, you could again attempt a redpoint day, as per usual, and follow that day with stamina training.

As you adapt to this increased climbing program, you could slowly increase the difficulty of the grades of routes from your third day on. Once you are back up to working harder routes, you could begin to do more tries in the day or decrease the rest time. It is crucial that you approach this change with caution and pay close attention to muscle strain or joint inflammation.

Choosing to decrease the rest day would allow you to follow a similar pattern as before, and also permit you to more quickly increase the difficulty in the problems you do. You could rotate your two climbing days around the rest-day pattern. For example, you would do a power day and a recovery day on your first two days, then a redpoint day and stamina day. After one day of rest, you would do another power day and recovery day, and then have two days of rest before a redpoint day and stamina day. It is crucial to injury prevention that you are very careful on the second power-training day to rest appropriately, even more than usual, and to decrease the number of tries initially.

Use the forms at the end of this chapter to outline your plans over the course of at least nine weeks. Having a picture of what you want to accomplish and the pace of progression can help you achieve your goals. It is important that the goals you outline are things that you are genuinely motivated to accomplish. Be reasonable with the amount of time commitment you make as well. Failing to keep up with your plan can leave you less motivated and generally less productive.

FORM 5	GOALS

Performance Goals

    1.

    2.

    3.

Progress Goals

    1. a)

        b)

        c)

    2. a)

        b)

        c)

    3. a)

        b)

        c)

FORM 6	YOUR PLAN

TYPE OF CYCLE

Interval Plan   Focused Interval Plan   Periodized Plan

NUMBER OF WEEKS

PRIORITY OF WEAKNESSES

Endurance   Power Endurance   Power   Stamina   Recovery en route

Grip strength   Back strength   Core strength   Upper-arm strength

Closed skills   Open skills   Footwork   Straight-arms   Hip shifts

DAYS PER WEEK OF CLIMBING

FORM 7	THE PLAN
Week	Activity for Each Climbing Session
WEEK 1	
WEEK 2	
WEEK 3	
WEEK 4	
WEEK 5	
WEEK 6	
WEEK 7	
WEEK 8	
WEEK 9	
WEEK 10	
WEEK 11	
WEEK 12	

Note: It is very important that you go into a power-training day with at least twenty-four hours' rest, and that you rest at least twelve hours after the session. If you have a high level of recovery, you can minimize your rest. If you have a lower level of recovery, it is better to rest more, decreasing your chances for injury.

Chapter 8

WHERE DOES TECHNIQUE FIT?

T here will always be different styles of climbers—those who are more power-ful versus those who are more technical. The key to improving overall perfor-mance is being able to adapt to the style most required throughout the route.

MOVEMENT

The human constraints in movement include strength, power, endurance, and flexi-bility. In other words, what you can successfully do is determined by your level of strength, the rate you can exert strength, the amount of repetition of movement you can execute, and the range of movement of your body. When this is related to climb-ing, your primary purpose is to move your body in interaction with the line of holds. Unfortunately, for every force there is a counterforce (or opposing force), which, in the climbing environment, is gravity. In addition to this force acting against your body, there are resistive forces within your body. Resistive forces include the tension of your muscles, the resistance of connective tissue to being stretched, and the contact of bones between two of your body segments. All of this makes climbing harder, but not impossible. These forces can be countered not just with increased strength or flex-ibility, but also by body position in movement and between movements—in other words, technique.

THE HIERARCHY OF LEARNING MOVEMENT PATTERNS

Technique is defined as a style of execution of a skill. This means that different indi-viduals may execute the movement in different ways and still have success. There are different levels of technique development, beginning with natural movement pat-terns adapted from other experiences and applied to that first route. As you experi-ence more routes and interact with other climbers, you develop new skills, such as dropknees and heel hooks, adding these to your repertoire of movement. Included in this chapter is a list of different body positions. For most climbers with a little experi-ence, many of these will not be new. There are, however, some details about these body positions and transitions, or movement patterns, that may be new.

The third level of technique development is where you attempt to understand when, where, and how to use these various movements. For example, you can identify more readily that the dropknee will work in a given place on a route, but not in another, because of the nature of the holds available and the angle of the route. This process is continually ongoing as you learn more movement patterns and gain experience on different terrain. It is generally at this phase of learning that people are considered to have "good" technique. "Good" technique often refers to climbing in such a way that it appears "effortless" or like a vertical dance. Whereas one can argue that success is success regardless of the style in which it is executed, the counterargument is that the lack of "good" technique will limit the optimal level of progress you can achieve. In this level of movement, you may be executing the skills in a more efficient manner, pushing more through the legs and pulling less with the arms. You can reach this level of technique without being aware of just how you know which positions to use; it is instinctive.

After mastering the application of movements, having a clear perspective of body size and shape relative to the configuration of the holds, you can then move to the next level of understanding. At this level, you can find the subtlety of the position or movement, making the difference between successful execution and trying again. This level in itself has stages of improved perceptiveness, ranging from more-exaggerated shifts in the hips to subtle pressure with the thumb on a hold. This stage of learning begins with the identification of when to apply the body position or transition.

The sport of climbing at present lacks awareness of these types of nuances in movement patterns. As climbers get closer and closer to the most difficult routes, some become increasingly aware of subtlety in movement, but other climbers are not sure what they do or don't do that makes the difference between success and failure. In sports such as figure skating and gymnastics, nuances of movement are analyzed by coaches. Subtle errors in the way the skill is performed are marked against the competitor. For some performers, these mistakes lead to failure in completing the skill, similar to climbing, where mistakes in nuances can lead to falling.

Imagine how much further the sport could go in terms of movement difficulty with a better understanding of the biomechanics of movement. If the best climbers in North America have limited understanding of the nuance of movements on V12 or V14, then awareness of this would enable them to do even harder moves. There is very limited knowledge in the understanding of movement, and this slows the progress of the sport. When Chris Sharma read an article describing his style of climbing as incorporating the outward flag, he wasn't sure if he actually applied that technique or not (*Rock & Ice*, August/September 1998). The irony at the time was that the editors of the piece were afraid they would not be able to find a photo depicting this particular move. When they went through the collection of photos of Chris, they found only two where he wasn't executing this particular movement.

A distinct picture of this hierarchy of technique development is depicted in position 6 on page 94. It shows the initial movement patterns being the compilation of what we know from other experiences. The natural instinct to grab holds and pull them toward the chest is often incorporated in this stage. A progression from this stage to the level of using techniques that involve turning sideways from the rock, as with dropknees and back steps, becomes a secondary phase of learning.

With these techniques—front steps, back steps, dropknees, heel hooks—you now start trying to figure out which is the most appropriate in what situation. The more one particular position and/or transition is used, the more information you know about it and the greater understanding of its application you have. Finally, you progress to an awareness of the subtlety of each movement. This gets developed more quickly with very difficult movements, where the nuance makes the difference between success and failure.

Jim Collins and Jim Logan—each with more than twenty years' experience—set out to attempt a sport route in Eldorado Canyon called *Captain Crunch* (5.13a). Both worked out a sequence and began the redpoint quest. During their subsequent breaks from working on the route, both did a few technique sessions and began to focus on making some changes in their style. When they did get back to the route, they tried resequencing their moves—or, as they called it, "Heatherizing" the route. Their sequence changed from twenty-seven moves to seventeen moves, and the route was shortly thereafter redpointed. Although both Jims had been climbing for many years, the application of new movement patterns to their project allowed them to decrease the overall energy expenditure on the route. Both could have done the route without learning and practicing new movement patterns, but maybe not as quickly and easily.

MOVEMENT PROGRESSION
A. **Instinctive approach**
  - what climbing means to a beginner
  - knowledge from previous experiences
  - trial and error
B. **Learning various techniques**

• dropknees	• wrapping	• crimping
• heel hooks	• gastoning	• open-handing
• heel/toe cams	• arm bars	• toeing in
• back steps	• hand jams	• smearing
• front steps	• finger locks	• edging
• high steps	• fist jams	• flagging

C. **Application of techniques**
  - efficient movement patterns
  - effective movement patterns
  - options for body position in transition
  - visualizing body size relative to holds
D. **Various nuances of movement**
  - push vs. pull with the toes
  - tightness in neck
  - pressure of grip
  - subtlety of thumb catch
  - hip tension in movement
  - opposition
  - shoulder rotation
  - wave of extension from toes to shoulder (toes, ankles, knees, hips, back, chest, reach)
  - body position in jumping (extending fully and turning as you go up, with a pop at the end)
  - rigidity in back relative to hip flexibility
  - hip shift, then upper body movement
  - momentum benefits and control

CLIMBING POSITIONS

Your individual physical strengths, knowledge, flexibility, and coordination tend to influence the types of movement patterns you frequently use when climbing. As previously outlined, insufficient back and shoulder strength will tend to force you to bring your feet higher during movement, making you more dependent on grip strength or core tension. The opposite is true if you have disproportionately strong back and shoulders. You will tend to rely more on pulling holds down rather than using higher feet on the route.

There are two basic components of climbing—hanging onto the holds and moving between the holds. These can also be referred to as resting/hanging positions and transitions. The art of climbing involves moving from one resting position, through a transition, to another resting position. As the level of difficulty increases, you may not be able to move to a rest position, but rather, be required to link transitions. The complexity of the sport arises with the difficulty of the transitions. Most of the time, you don't fail in a hanging position, but rather, in the transition—because transitions tend to require more work than does maintaining the hanging positions.

Making the transition from one hold to the next can usually be completed in more than one way. If you think about it, you can probably remember a route where you and your partner climbed through the sequence quite differently. Generally the difference can be seen in the transitions as opposed to the holds. Your sequence was more effective for you. Your partner's sequence was better for him or her. Part of what distinguishes the most effective sequence is your personal muscle strengths. If you have a very strong core but a less powerful upper arm, you may execute the move differently than a climber with the exact opposite in muscle-strength development. For you, the most efficient way is to use the strongest and biggest muscle group available for the movement. However, your plan to improve in the technique arena should also incorporate increasing your upper-arm strength, giving you more options for the implementation of movements.

Some of you will be very skilled at getting into resting positions after the transitions, and some will be very good with the transitions. Fewer of you will be good at both. The biggest benefit to being skillful at both is that you save a lot of energy, by climbing with momentum and by relying more on the work of fewer muscles. When you watch someone climb and they seem to be flowing from one move to the next, they are probably good at both transitions and hanging positions.

Analyzing Body Positions

The following illustrations depict primarily hanging positions, though some may be more efficient than others. For clarification of other techniques, refer to *How to Rock Climb* by John Long, or *Performance Rock Climbing* by Dale Goddard and Udo Neumann. Use these illustrations to identify body positions you use or don't use. Start to consider why these positions haven't been incorporated into your repertoire of movement. It is beneficial to try to imitate some of these movement patterns in your warm-up climbs. If the positions seem awkward, it may indicate that it is a pattern you do not incorporate frequently in your own style of climbing.

You could also videotape yourself climbing a variety of routes on different angles and with different sequences to get a feel for how you actually do perform movements. There are crucial things to examine when looking at a body position or movement. The first thing you want to consider is that all climbing movement either works or doesn't work because of the forces acting on the body, and the counterforce of the body on the rock or holds. This takes us back to physics class and the concepts of forces, opposing forces, and levers. To keep things simple, simply notice where the feet are in relation to the hand. If the handhold is a side pull, the outside leg will be higher to counter the force of the body as it wants to swing around from the side pull. If the handhold is horizontal, there is less likelihood of this problem, and the foot may stay lower and more underneath your body.

The second thing to watch for is where the hips are relative to the hand the climber is hanging from. Third, consider how the torso is positioned. Is it facing the rock or away from the rock? Is the arm bent? Is the back arched? Are the hips in over the feet, or is the butt drooping? What part of the shoe is on the foothold? Are you using the toe or the upper section of the shoe?

If you can illustrate your typical movement patterns on a piece of paper and compare them to the movements described in this section, it may give you some new ideas for sequencing in the future. The positions outlined in this chapter are specifically designed to be efficient, and may not in all instances be effective. When you lack the grip strength required to hang a hold, you may bend the elbow, incorporating more upper-arm strength in the total force of the grip. Although this may be less efficient, it may be the only way for you to successfully complete the action. This is where effective movement patterns are more important than efficient movement patterns.

After I can successfully do the transitions, I always go back to the same problems and try to complete them in ways I could not do previously. For example, I may work specifically on performing the movements with straight arms. In other situations, I sometimes start to eliminate the footholds, forcing myself to climb more powerfully through the upper arm and less through my core strength. I happen to be a better core-tension climber than a powerful climber. The ideal is to be good at both and to know how to alternate between the two styles.

RESTING (OR HANGING) POSITIONS

POSITION 1	FRONT STEP

In a front step, you place the front part of the shoe, or the big-toe area of the shoe, on the hold. In this position, the leg is often rotated outward so the knee points away from the center of the body. The force on the foothold is exerted through the toe, upward following the line of the ankle, knee, and hip.

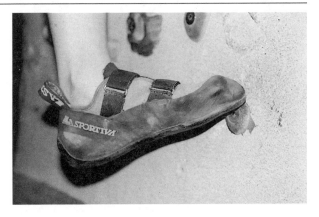

POSITION 2	BACK STEP

The back step involves placing the outside part of the shoe, near the inside of the big toe, on the hold—as opposed to the front and inside of the big toe on the foothold. In this position, you have your hip close to the wall, usually with the body facing sideways to the wall. This position allows you to stand through your leg and bring the opposite hand lower than shoulder height—in other words, to lock off more easily. This foot position can be seen in the photo of transition 13 on page 107.

POSITION 3	HIGH STEP

The high step involves placing the foot in a high front step and shifting the hips over the foot. You are then in the position of sitting over the one foot, which is stepped high. You can use the hands to balance and support a full extension. In some instances, the foot placement can be up and outward from the body.

POSITION 4   OUTSIDE FLAG

Flagging allows you to counterbalance forces pulling your body off in a rotational position, known among climbers as barndooring. A flag position can be used with an inside leg or an outside leg, and can also be effective in limiting the number of required foot changes.

POSITION 5   INSIDE FLAG

The difference between an outside flag and an inside flag is the placement of the leg. An inside flag places the leg between the front step foot and the rock. The motion of the leg is still pressing upward and toward the rock to prevent the barn-door action.

POSITION 6   OUTWARD FLAG

An outward flag involves flagging the leg outward behind the body, enabling a more direct upward motion on steep terrain. Overhanging rock requires an upward and outward motion with the upper body. Doing this type of action can cause a loss of body tension when you latch the destination hold. The outward swing of the body is countered by the leg's being in a counterbalance position on the completion of the move.

POSITION 7   DROPKNEE

Dropknees have a very useful purpose, particularly on very big moves or steep angles and on slopers. This technique uses one leg to hold your hip into the wall, while the opposing foot is in front of you or directly underneath you. This body position prevents a barn-door scenario as you reach in front of yourself or directly upward. The fundamental difference between the dropknee and a back step is that in a back step, the foot is on top of the hold, whereas in a dropknee, the foot pushes against the side of the hold. This is demonstrated in the photo.

As seen from the example, dropknees are helpful in moving to holds directly above the climber or in front of the climber. Reaching for holds be-

(continued)

POSITION 7	DROPKNEE *(continued)*

hind the climber is more difficult from a dropknee due to the decreased range of flexibility with the foot high and behind the body.

In some situations, as seen above, the dropknee requires a stable hip position, as movement through the hips will cause the body to loose the opposition in the feet, and the climber then comes out of the position. This is usually the case in a strenuous dropknee, where the legs and feet are fairly extended or the opposition is tenuous. In a less strenuous dropknee, you can stand up through the hips and maintain some pressure through the feet.

POSITION 8	KNEE BARS

A knee bar is used to hold your hips into the rock or wall and take some of the work away from the arms. Getting into this position requires that the thigh, just above the knee, is placed against a protrusion of the rock and cammed into place by pressure exerted into it with toes of the same foot. The subtlety to making a knee bar work is in the direction of pull from the hips and the position of the upper body. On less-stable knee bars, the upper body may need to be leaning into the thigh. However, some knee bars are so good that you can let go with both hands to rest.

POSITION 9   HEEL/TOE CAMS

A heel/toe cam is used to hold your body into the rock. This requires a push and pull from the foot. While the toe pulls outward on the rock holding it into position, the heel is cammed into position with the resulting force. This can allow the climber to make movements while being held into the rock, limiting the required body tension.

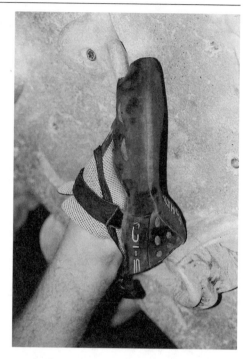

POSITION 10   HEEL HOOKS

You would use a heel hook to hold your body into the rock and to give you some height on a move where there was an obvious high foot, and no really useful feet lower. The heel is pulled inward to the body, causing the knee to rotate upward and outward. This brings the groin close to the foot in the heel-hook position, allowing you to reach the next hold. Heel hooks are also useful in a lower position if there is a reason to pull with the foot rather than push through the toe.

POSITION 11   CRIMPING

Crimping involves placing the tips of your fingers on the handhold and bending the second knuckle. This allows the thumb to cross over the top of the index finger.

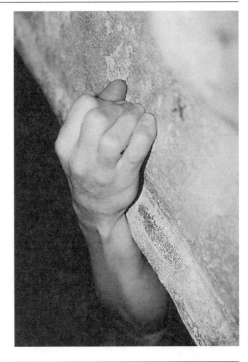

POSITION 12   OPEN HAND

To open-hand a hold, simply drape your hand over the top of the hold. You can open-hand a hold with just the tips of the fingers or with the length of the fingers.

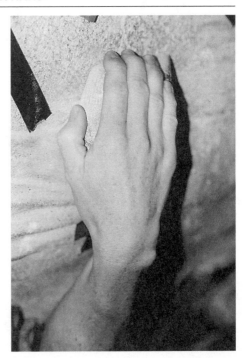

POSITION 13   GASTONING

In a gaston position, your thumb points downward and your little finger is upward. The palm faces away from you as you push outward on a hold. Usually the elbow is forced outward and away from you, too. A high-risk gaston position is pictured on page 145.

POSITION 14   WRAPPING

When you wrap a hold, you may do so with either the hand or the lower portion of the arm. In the accompanying photo, the back of the hand is against the rock, and the hand drapes over the hold. Similarly, the elbow or lower arm may be draped over a hold, if large enough.

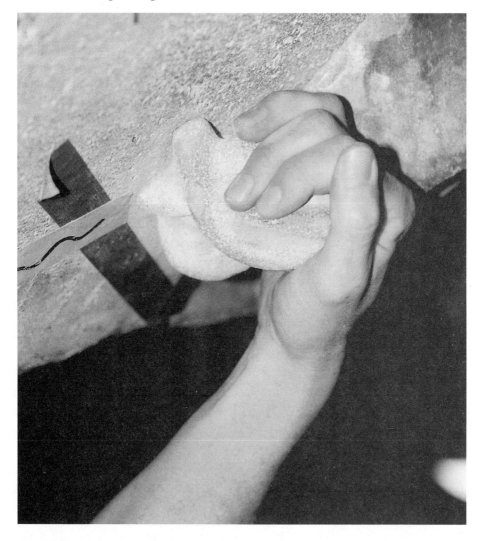

TRANSITIONS

The following examples attempt to describe the nuances of some forms of movement. Using the depictions below, try these moves and discover the kinesthetic differences between them. Prior to attempting the body positions and transitions described in this section, consider the comments in the above section and apply similar principles.

TRANSITION 1   **HIP SHIFT VS. BENT ARM**

Although you may begin in a similar body position, the execution of this transition can be accomplished in a few different ways. In *A*, the pull is through the arm as the reach to the next hold is executed. In *B*, Tommy is arching through the hips and keeping the arm extended during the reach. In *B*, he can thus gain more height and use less arm strength and more core tension, making this movement efficient and generally more effective. The telltale sign is that Tommy arches through the back in a straight-arm move.

A.   **B.**

TRANSITION 2   SHOULDER ROLLS

The position in this photo depicts a straight-arm, while the left hand reaches above the body. In the movement, notice that the body turns toward the right arm, and the chest rotates to the wall. Rather than bend the arm for height, Tommy rolls his chest over the arm and levers upward to reach the next hold. A similar position is demonstrated in transition 6 on page 102. In these photos, you can again see the chest roll toward the arm as he reaches.

TRANSITION 3   SAGGING BUTT

The following comparison illustrates the difference between a climber who allows the butt to droop while doing movements versus one who tucks his rump inward. The main difference is in the strength of core tension and the subsequent height available to the climber.

TRANSITION 4	**HEAD TUCK**

In the photos accompanying the high-risk body positions (page 145), Tommy demonstrates both the maintenance of back rigidity by tucking his head in toward the rock and, conversely, his head falling outward. The head tucked in, as seen in the lower photo, allows him to use more back in the move. In the top photo, the head is dropped backward, making the position even more difficult to do.

TRANSITION 5	**PULLING THE BELLY BUTTON IN TOWARD THE SPINE**

This is a trick discovered in a Pilates session. To incorporate deeper abdominal muscles into core-tension movements, think about pulling your belly button in toward your spine. If the move was low percentage before, you may notice that it has suddenly become easier for two reasons. The first is that the action of pulling your tummy in creates an elongation of the spine—hence, the object of your reach is not as far away. The second benefit is the incorporation of deeper muscle tissue in the movement. If you have trouble figuring this out, try yelling during the difficult move and you have done this action.

TRANSITION 6	**WAVE OF EXTENSION**

A key part of efficiency in movement is maintaining the momentum carried from one hold to the next. This momentum is initiated in the first move and can be carried along with the help of gravity. To accomplish this, you need to allow the movement to begin with the placement of the foot. You then transfer the weight to the foot, push through the ankles, extending the knees, moving the hips, arching the back, turning the waist and chest, and reaching through the arm to the next hold. Relaxing this body position and allowing gravity to pull diverts the momentum to the next transition, which, in this example, is a pivot.

(continued)

TRANSITION 6 **WAVE OF EXTENSION** *(continued)*

TRANSITION 7 **DEADPOINT, THE ARC**

Dynos are a favorite of many climbers and are required on certain routes. In Smith Rock, Oregon, there is a classic 5.11b called *Toxic* that requires a dynamic move for the tall guys. The nature of a dyno is dependent upon the start position, the length of the throw, and the holds used. The typical classifications include shapes similar to the following letters. The letter C dyno shows a low starting position, an outward arc up, with an inward latch. The feet remain on the starting holds. This dyno has the body move in the arc of a C, hence its name.

(continued)

TRANSITION 7   **DEADPOINT, THE ARC (continued)**

TRANSITION 8   **THE FLAG DYNO**

The dyno that involves the use of the outward flag is known as an *I* dyno. With one leg extended outward behind you, your hips begin out and away from the rock. Move dynamically upward with the hips following a relatively straight line upward, tracing the letter *I*. The initiation of this movement requires more power through the back and upper arms. Less work is required at the end of the move because there is no force pulling the lower body outward from the rock. Therefore, if the move involves a small, hard-to-latch finishing hold, this dyno is more effective.

TRANSITION 9   **THE INWARD DEADPOINT**

When you do a dyno on steep terrain where you must pull yourself inward to the rock at the initiation and then directly upward, it traces an arc inward and up. The key to success with this move is to latch the finishing hold and to maintain feet on the starting footholds.

TRANSITION 10 THE CURVE DYNO

If you consider the arc dyno again, the nature of the dyno changes when the move is longer and the feet cut loose, momentum carrying them in an outward and upward arc. This dyno takes the shape of the letter *S* as the feet swing outward.

The benefit to being able to jump well is obviously not just in getting to the next hold, but also in a progressive attitude of commitment to movements. Friend, climber, and sculptor Ian Powell from Boulder is one of the best jumpers in climbing. Fittingly, he attended a junior team practice and taught the juniors how to jump. Prior to the clinic, one of the team members would hesitate on any long move and eventually not succeed in doing the move. After a session with Ian, this particular junior would jump for anything. (Remember, though: everything in moderation.)

TRANSITION 11   **SIDEWAYS JUMPING**

Sideways jumping is a form of dyno or explosive upward and sideways movement. The setup for this motion is similar to the C dyno or jump. The feet are up high under the hands, with perhaps the foot opposite the direction of jump out to the side a little more. The climber then creates some momentum going in a sideward direction, using the outward foot to push the body toward the destination hold. The arms push the handhold down and to the side of the body as you release and move sideways and upward to the hold.

TRANSITION 12   **SUBTLETY IN GRIP**

It is interesting to play with various ways to grip holds and to note which of your fingers provide the most strength. Some people prefer the index and middle fingers in two finger pockets, while others declare the ring and middle as the best option. Although you may think you would use all fingers on an edge that allows for them, you may discover otherwise if the depth of the edge allows for only a half a pad.

Try different holds and find out your own preferences. Due to the structure of the hand and its musculature, as well as training, certain positions are stronger for some people but not for others. The use of the thumb is something every climber should try to incorporate as much as possible. The thumb can provide a more secure grip and assist in the maintenance of the position for a longer movement.

TRANSITION 13   ONE-FOOT CLIMBING IN A BACK STEP

Climbing with only one foot on is more difficult in most cases than using two feet on the wall. The predominant difference is in the balance at the initiation of the move and the finish of the move. Because the body position changes, so does the required balance. Therefore, often the foot provides the best assistance if it is in the better position for execution and is moved quickly at the completion of the movement.

TRANSITION 14   EXTENDED ONE-FOOT ROCK OVER

When you have a foot extended out to the side and your handholds are more directly above you, the motion requires that you pull and push the handholds toward you and then away to the side of you. This allows your hips to shift toward and up over the extended foot. This movement can be difficult to learn because it requires upper-body motion at the same time as an incorporation of the lower body. During the pull through the upper body, the leg is pulling the hips inward, and the hips are shifting toward the foot. Coordination of these different elements is key to successful execution of the transition.

TRANSITION 15   **EXTENDED ONE-FOOT HIP ROLL**

In some instances, when the next handhold is not out toward the extended foot, you can save some arm strength and use more core tension by rolling your hips upward and outward from the wall to reach your destination. In this instance, the leg is providing a downward pressure on the foothold to sustain the body tension as the abdominal and oblique muscles work to rotate the torso, rolling the chest over the arm that is hanging on. This extends the opposite shoulder upward toward the hold. Thus, the climber does not bend the arm in order to reach.

These are just a few of the many nuances involved in execution of movement. A dancer once said to me that all dancers come to dance with their own little movement pattern—it is different for everyone. For her, it was a tilt of the head. So it is with climbers.

CLIMBING STYLES

Technique is an important aspect of performance. It can assist the climber in compensating for lack of pure strength. In the sport of climbing, it is difficult to define technique. There are numerous climbers with different body types who also demonstrate different styles of climbing. For example, climbers such as Katie Brown rely more on static strength, while other climbers—Greg Loh and Chris Sharma, for example—are well known for their dynamic power. A comparison of these climbers' body types illustrates the different anthropometric definitions. The static climbers tend to be leaner, with an endomorphic shape, while the more powerful, dynamic climbers would be better classified as mesomorphic in stature. Ultimately, this is a genetic factor that cannot be varied greatly by the individual. The significance is how this factors in with the style of climbing best suited to the individual.

Climbers with a mesomorphic body type tend to excel on shorter-duration routes with more-powerful cruxes. The endomorphic types can perform better on longer routes. Part of this is simply biomechanics, and some of it is actual physiology. With shorter, more powerful lever arms, the individual can perform more explosive movements, generating greater power because the contraction is performed over a shorter distance and thus less time. If you are a shorter, bulkier climber, then you also probably have a greater portion of fast-twitch muscle fibers. These are thicker than slow-twitch fibers and generally react more quickly. On the downside, these fibers also have fewer mitochondria, the powerhouses of cells, meaning that they don't deal with aerobic situations as well.

To further illustrate the differences, think about a taller person doing bent-knee sit-ups and the increased range the body must move through to reach the knees compared to a shorter person doing the same action. Similarly, a shorter body can move through this range more quickly and explosively.

Those of you with the endomorphic body types probably have a greater portion of slow-twitch muscle fibers and can manage an aerobic situation much more efficiently. This doesn't mean that you should revert to one style of climbing over another. These muscle fibers can, according to some sport scientists, be trained to behave more like the slow-twitch fibers or more like fast-twitch fibers. A third type of fiber called the red fast twitch has properties of both of the other two fibers. You also have a portion of these within your muscles. It is thought that it is these fibers that adapt to training stress and subsequently demonstrate the properties needed for performance.

The best solution to the question of what technique or style is best is to be proficient at both styles, even though you may be naturally better at one than the other. This means training the style you find more difficult to execute both mentally and physically. If you have a shorter, more powerful physique, you may be forced to improve your core tension, enabling you to maintain tension while fully extended because you probably will be in this position frequently. Mentally, you may prefer this static approach. As a result, your ability to move dynamically and to powerfully use your more genetically inclined body has declined. This limits your options in ways to do moves and routes. In physiological terms, you will need to work more on power endurance, enabling you to do more than fifteen moves before you pump off the route.

On the other hand, you may be less powerful and more technical, excelling on static movements with body tension and precise footwork. Improving your dynamic climbing and precision while moving faster will be a challenge. The benefits will be improved power and commitment to moves. The mental and physical aspects of your climbing performance will benefit.

With this new awareness of technique, incorporate the practice of one physical technique, either a resting position or a transition, into each warm-up on a daily basis. The point is not merely to do the technique, but to execute it well. To this end, ensure that your partner critiques your movement and provides feedback. If it is difficult to find a partner willing and able, use a system board or a video camera. You will be able to feel if you are executing the move appropriately on the system board. Pay close attention to the change in feel of the position.

A video camera is an excellent tool for assessing your climbing performance. Having yourself videotaped while climbing on both easier and more-difficult routes allows you to see what your transitions are like and whether you find the resting po-

sitions or not. Comparing yourself to another climber on the same route can illustrate different styles of climbing. This awareness is an essential part of knowing your own style.

For my own definition of technique, I always think of "good" technique as being defined by my husband, Nick. His body automatically moves into the most balanced position possible. If the problem or move does not lend itself to balance, then he quickly moves through the sequence into a move that does allow for a rest position. It is this fluidity in his movement that I appreciate. Conversely, unlike Tommy Caldwell, Nick cannot control the momentum of his hips as easily.

There is a route in Rifle called *Tomfoolery*. It is graded 5.14b, and consists of a three-bolt section of 5.12+ climbing to a good knee-bar rest. Then you climb through a ten-move V9 or V10 to continuous 5.13b/c climbing for another four bolts. At the end of the 5.13b/c section, you are under a roof with a right high step and reach out behind you with your right hand to an undercling. You then spin around and look outward from the rock to the road, matching your feet and stemming your body between the features under the roof. Nick would stay in this rest for four or five minutes, trying to depump his arms before heading into the next V9 or V10 section. The final 5.12 section would come next, if he wasn't too pumped to climb through it to the anchors.

The beauty illustrated in Nick's ability to move through his hips on the relatively easier sections and then shrug his shoulders and power through the big pulls of the bouldery parts is close to the ideal for climbing hard routes. This was not natural for him, though, and it took months of practice. Changing your style takes time, trial, and—probably for most of us—a bit of error, too.

Chapter 9

MENTAL
TRAINING TIPS

Success in any sport requires a strong sense of confidence, a positive attitude, and the ability to focus attention on the task at hand. The mental control required under physical exertion at your limit is what often separates world-class athletes from the mainstream. These are skills that can be developed and can be instrumental in improving climbing performance.

All athletes come to their sport with some talent. For some, it is in the physical realm; for others, the psychological domain. The most successful athletes are those who have natural physical talent for the sport of choice *and* the mental capacity as well. Unfortunately, for some, mental training is the most difficult to measure and to do. In many situations, you will not recognize that it is a mental aspect that is limiting your performance. You may perform for many years and never realize your true potential because you do not recognize the mental limitations of your performance.

There are some telltale signs you can use to identify mental limitations. Spending a lot of time on a route and yet seeing diminished gains is one sign. Another is throwing yourself at the route, trying again and again, continually increasing your level of frustration. A third obvious sign is always saying take or grabbing draws rather than climbing to failure on redpoint and on-sight tries. Even things you say prior to getting on the route indicate your mental attitude toward your performance.

There are numerous mental battles in the climbing realm—fear of failure, fear of success, fear of pain or injury, arousal control, focus, slumps, injuries, expectations, confidence, and perfectionism. Any and all of these challenges will diminish your overall performance. And you have probably experienced a day where none of these things were present and everything flowed and you performed your best. That is the kind of day you want to keep having.

The main source of information for these exercises was the enlightening book *Thinking Body, Dancing Mind,* in which authors Chungliang Al Huang and Jerry Lynch approach sport from the Tao perspective. This wonderful book provided many exercises and ideas for improving climbing performance and everyday life.

FEAR

Fear is the root of many climbers' limitations. In the domain of traditional climbing or mountaineering, this is a relatively valid feeling. However, in sport climbing, the focus is not on the protection of the route, but rather, the physical movement and strength of the climber. That is not to say that sport climbers don't experience fear—they do, and once it has reared its ugly head, the climber is distracted from the moves at hand. The first step in combating this fear is to identify it and recognize what it is. Is it a fear of falling or of failing? Is it a fear of success? Is it a fear of injury or of an unsafe belay?

Once the fear has been identified, determine if it is a reasonable one. On most sport routes, there is little realistic fear of injury, unless you don't trust your belayer. Fear of failing or succeeding on a route is a natural feeling, though perhaps unnecessary. Failure and success are concepts that can be interpreted in different contexts. For myself, I succeed just leading to the first bolt because I hate leading and I've overcome a major fear in doing it. If failure for you means not redpointing or onsighting, you may need to change your understanding of that word. What difference does it really make if you don't do the route? What difference does it make if you don't try? It may make a difference to you personally, but it really does not matter to others.

Fear of falling can be just that, a fear of free-falling. Closer examination may indicate that it is really a fear of being out of control. Once you are in the air, you can't do anything until you hit the end of the rope. As I struggled to overcome my fear and tried taking falls on routes, I came to realize I really wasn't afraid of the fall. I was afraid of the anticipation of the fall. When I could feel the pump growing in my forearms and experience the bombardment of negative messages, the fear would become overwhelming. I would become paralyzed and invariably try to grab the draw below me or down climb to it. It also always involved a lot of screaming.

The trick is to do something about it before you leave the ground. Once the fear has been identified and classified and it has been determined that there is no real physical danger, the next step involves limiting the amount the fear affects your performance. There are numerous tricks to accomplish this, and not all the ideas work for everybody. Try different ones at different times, and determine which seems the most effective for you and keep developing it.

Many of the information and exercises in this section have been adapted from meditative exercises found in other sources. The first step in dealing with the mental element of climbing is to identify a limitation imposed by your thoughts and then to counter it before you leave the ground.

MENTAL TRICKS

MENTAL TRICK 1 **PACK UP YOUR FEAR**

Climbing a great route in the Virgin River Gorge called *The Mentor* (5.12b) involves coming out a couple of really steep roofs. Due to the nature of its steepness, the bolts are well spaced for my taste, and the route itself is quite pumpy. This route had me in tears the first time I climbed it and went swinging out into the air on a top rope. But a year later, I was in the same area looking for a 12b to climb. Leading it seemed just as scary as top roping, so leading I was. The only thing that helped me tie into the rope and get on the thing was sitting at the base of the climb and visualizing putting my fear in a backpack and zipping it closed. I would then climb through the lower part of the route, get to the steep roof, and begin to feel it creep back at me. I tried taking the falls I was so afraid of, and that helped me climb through those sections a little better. But it seemed like there was a time limit on how long the fear would stay zipped in the backpack at the base of the route.

Some coaches recommend talking to your fear, giving it an image and facing it. By talking to your fear, you can regain some of the power that it is draining from you. Recognize that the feeling of fear is a way for your subconscious to attempt to protect you from danger. Recognizing the fear and accepting the danger, with a consciousness of risk and intense focus, can help you climb with your fear. And then put it where it belongs so you can move along to the next step—climbing without it.

Recognize your fear and give yourself the power overcome it or to leave it on the ground.

MENTAL TRICK 2 **CHASE FEAR AWAY WITH HUMOR**

Humor can go a long way toward decreasing your arousal level and creating a fun, positive experience. Fear of failure and success are best managed with humor, because really, what is the worst that can happen? If you succeed, you need to go find another challenge—and if you don't, who cares what those other humans think. All humans make mistakes and look like Neanderthals at some point or another. Being able to joke about being afraid helps you to accept your fear and not compound it with expectations from others. Those Neanderthals can be supportive if they know that someone needs it. Be able to laugh at yourself and keep a healthy perspective of success and failure.

I recall one fall being in the Red River Gorge, climbing at *The Motherlode* on a brisk day. I was watching and cheering on a fellow climber who was working on a 5.12c. The route went up a steep section on the right side of the amphitheater and had quite a feeling of exposure to it. As with all the routes at *The Motherlode*, the space between the last bolt and the anchors is generally significant. This is the point on all the routes where the pump is also the greatest. As I watched this woman struggle with her pump and the unknown sequence, her fear also became an added burden. Those of us on the ground hollered our encouragement, telling her she was "doing fine" and all those ridiculous things spectators yell. She was not sold. Her retort came in the form of expression of her fear. She was clucking like the chicken she felt herself to be, as she continued to struggle to hang on and avoid the inevitable whipper. How much she was benefiting from her humor is hard to say, but I certainly enjoyed it then, and have thought of it often when I am feeling the same overwhelming fear. I certainly will support any climber out there pushing their weaknesses to that extent.

MENTAL TRICK 3   **BLOCK IT**

The best ascents I've ever made are when I've managed to just focus on each move of the route and nothing else. When mentally and physically challenged to the max, there is no room for fear in my thoughts. This can be accomplished on easier routes by rehearsing the moves in your head until the route can be continuously rehearsed with no interruption.

Rehearse moves until there is no room for other thoughts.

MENTAL TRICK 4   **GAIN CONTROL**

Falling or failing on a route can leave you feeling vulnerable and potentially out of control. The best solution is to regain that sensation of control. One way to accomplish this is to go into the gym or to a warm-up and decide how many falls you are planning to take. Then climb the route, focusing on the movements and the climbing. In a movement, make a split-second decision to take a fall. Don't hang on the holds, check your belayer/knot, or do anything. You should be in the process of reaching for another hold or moving a foot—and then just miss the next hold or let go. Scream if you have to. Screaming can help you feel a lot better.

Control the situation by deciding when and where you will fall.

MENTAL TRICK 5   **TURN "FAILURE" INTO SUCCESS**

Putting together the information from your "failures" can lead to success. Reward yourself for finding your weaknesses and determining how to work on them. Remember that although failure on a route is disappointing, it need not be devastating, but rather, enlightening.

Failure is a prerequisite to success. Stop, listen, learn!!!

MENTAL TRICK 6   **MOVE OUT OF YOUR COMFORT ZONE**

Success requires that you feel uncomfortable and that you experience failure. Although failure may not lead to injury, it can mean a certain level of embarrassment. Failure is not the only form of discomfort that you may experience. Fear is certainly another example of discomfort. However, without fear, success would be limited. Unless you push yourself past your fear, you cannot move to another level of difficulty. Recognize that trying and failing are a large part of the process to success that everyone must endure. This is the best means of dealing with these uncomfortable feelings.

You may also feel compelled by others to perform well, or you may experience expressions of jealousy from peers about your performance compared to their own. Many of us are drawn to this sport because of the social interaction and interdependence element between climber and belayer. The best partners are always the ones who motivate and support your performance regardless of their own. Mike Caldwell (a.k.a. Tommy's dad) has expressed the importance of the energy that transmits through the rope from belayer to climber. A supportive partner is felt even when no words are spoken. Putting peers who are not supportive out of your mind is a crucial step. The people who really matter are the friends who support you regardless of performance.

Moving out of the comfort zone also means to physically work hard and to repeatedly try new ways of doing things. In most situations, this means climbing when your tips are sore and your muscles ache. For some climbers, the physical comfort level isn't as affected as the mental comfort zone. But success means moving out of both of these elements of comfort. It means putting yourself in a position where you will tend to fail more and focus less. But you will improve—not all at once, but definitely with time. With time, it will also become easier to tax yourself in this way.

Moving out of your comfort zone is a step toward expanding the realm of what you feel comfortable doing.

AROUSAL, PERCEPTIONS, AND EXPECTATIONS

Arousal is necessary for anyone to do anything. It is the element that raises your blood pressure, increases your circulation, delivers more oxygen to the muscles, and helps generate the required contractions. It can also be that thing that causes your heart to race so fast that you feel sick, and makes your legs shake so bad that your feet come off the footholds. Maintaining the optimum arousal level for performance requires practice.

Arousal is induced by our perceptions of what may happen and what should happen. These perceptions you have about the weather, the environment, and your readiness for the route allow you to create an expectation. Perceptions lead to expectations, and expectations can influence your arousal. You are expecting a certain performance, a feel for how hard things should feel. When something doesn't meet your expectation, your level of arousal quickly jumps up. In some situations, this may help you hang on. In most, if the elevated level remains high, you get more tired more quickly, you make more mistakes, and you have snowball effect until you fall.

AROUSAL MANAGEMENT

Maintaining the right arousal, not too excited but enough of a psych to meet the intensity of the route, requires creating as much control of the situation as possible, acknowledging what you can't control and accepting it. The accepting-it part is the most difficult, but there are ways to make that happen. The following ideas may help you to maintain the appropriate level of arousal for a given redpoint or on-sight.

MENTAL TRICK 7   **SAY IT**

If you know it's a pretty hot day and that such conditions are not optimal for you, say it out loud. Accept that the temperature might affect your performance, and then leave it. If you just think it, without acknowledging that you can't change it, as soon as your hand starts to slide on the sloper, your heart will pick up its pace, your panic will start, and the beginning of the end is close behind. Stating that it is hot and that the heat might affect your performance allows you to set a reasonable expectation—for example, that your hand may slide on that sloper. Rather than the panic, your reaction will be to move off it and leave it behind, without leaving your composure with it.

The expectation is the thing you can always control. With a reasonable expectation, you can maintain the appropriate level of arousal more readily. If you feel awkward stating it, then write it down, but the key is to believe what you say or write. Don't be afraid to say that you can do the route, but likewise, don't be afraid to acknowledge you might not. Your bottom line is to try your hardest.

Consciously recognize your expectations prior to performing.

MENTAL TRICK 8   **FIGHT FATIGUE**

At the end of just about every climbing day, you experience some level of fatigue. Angry messages from your muscles compel you to stop, go home, and soak in a hot bath. It is imperative that you learn to ignore messages about fatigue and focus on the moves before you! As you prepare for a route and climb through the moves, visualize your muscles tightening and relaxing on your command. Those not in use are relaxed but ready for action. Those in contraction are assisting in the movements. Know that you are not using 100 percent of your muscles' potential, and that what you have in reserve is regenerating and preparing for the next series of moves. Learn to recognize the messages that indicate potential injury and to distinguish them from those of fatigue.

Narrow your focus to the moves ahead of you rather than the fatigue within you.

FOCUS AND CONFIDENCE

The clarity that you gain from stating your expected performance outcome provides a better level of confidence and focus for a route. Without focus or confidence, you had better stick to things in your mental comfort zone and out of your physical comfort zone. Focus can be trained using meditation and yoga techniques designed for the way you function. If, for example, you are easily distracted and find that your thoughts move speedily from one topic to another, you are not likely to have success thinking of nothing. Success for those of you with rapidly developing thoughts is to allow your thoughts to focus on a task.

If you find it rather easy to allow your mind to think of nothing, developing your focus skills for a route may be a little easier. However, a more laid-back approach may not be as beneficial in a competition or perceived competitive arena. The excessive external stimuli may not allow your normal calm to prevail, and may in fact hinder your focus.

Confidence is a much harder skill to develop. It comes from happiness with your experiences and performances. Confidence cannot be given; it is a perception of your own abilities, and thus requires you to create it. You may disagree, and argue that when your partner yells encouragement, you do in fact believe that person and try harder. The counterargument is that you chose to believe your partner from what you know of yourself, your ability, your partner, and when he or she gives inspiration.

Thus, in order to develop your confidence, you must think positively about your abilities and experiences. For example, you could approach a competition with the attitude that you cannot make finals because of the high performance levels of the competitors. In this situation, you probably will not make finals. Conversely, you could approach the same event with the perspective that the qualifiers are within your on-sight level, and you expect to be able to on-sight them. This positive approach makes it more likely for you to climb well. Your competition is against yourself, and your attitude is positive.

Being successful means having confidence in your ability to realize success.

FOCUSING TOOLS

The following exercises are designed to assist you in developing your ability to maintain a high level of focus during a difficult redpoint or on-sight or perhaps in a competitive environment. It will take more than one or two tries to determine the tools that best suit you and to make these a regular part of your climbing routine. Thus, it is best to rehearse different tricks during different sessions and at the end of the practice. Describe in your journal whether you felt you had managed to maintain a good level of focus or not.

MENTAL TRICK 9	**VISUALIZATION**

Find a quiet place for yourself to sit or lie down and relax. Start by taking ten deep breaths. With each breath, concentrate on breathing the air into your lungs, filling your lungs out toward your back and upper neck. As you can feel the oxygen filling into your lungs, imagine it trickling through your arteries and running out from your lungs in all directions, toward your feet and hands, your head, and the sides of your body. Recognize the feeling of calm you are experiencing. Maintain the breathing pattern.

When you feel relaxed, bring your mind to the route or competition. Visualize the route. Progress through the route from the ground to the top. You want to see each hand- and foothold, to see yourself getting the hold and moving to the next hold, moving your foot to the next foothold. Climb the route in your mind at least twice before you physically get up and move to the route.

After this level of relaxation, you need to increase your arousal again by doing some deep breathing, preparing for the oxygen debt that is about to occur. You can also forcefully pump your arms out in front of you, preparing them for movement. Sustaining the appropriate level of arousal is essential to good performance.

This activity can also be practiced anytime, anywhere. It assures you of the sequence you plan to use for a redpoint and creates a positive image of your ability to complete the route, improving your confidence. In most cases, if you are not ready to do the route, this will be a difficult task to perform, because you will stumble through the sequence or recognize that you don't remember the foot sequence. That just means you can expect not to do the route, and you can go back to it and know what you need to figure out. Remember that the route isn't over until you've clipped the anchors, so sequence in the clipping of the anchors, too.

MENTAL TRICK 10   POSITIVE VISUALIZATION

Visualize a sequence on a route where you have been having problems. Repeat the visualization process as you successfully climb through the problem area. Re-create this positive image repetitively. It requires that you commit to a sequence of moves *and* that you imagine yourself successfully climbing through those moves. With each attempt, make positive statements about your performance on the route. The fundamental difference between this exercise and the one described above is the positive images and affirmations about your performances.

MENTAL TRICK 11   ELIMINATE THE DISTRACTIONS

One of the most difficult things to do when climbing is to eliminate the negative messages that come into your head as you progress or try to progress up a route or problem. The hold feels greasy. The hold feels much harder than the last time. Thoughts like these are guaranteed ways to limit your chances for success. But it is natural to experience these messages, unless you learn to ignore them.

Again, in a relaxed state, imagine yourself climbing through your boulder problem or route. Recognize in your mind the things that are happening around you—the sounds of other climbers, the clouds of chalk, the smell of climbing shoes and of sweaty bodies, even the noises of friends giving encouragement. Now, as you see yourself getting ready to go, to touch the starting holds, block those things out. Your vision includes only the holds you are on; your hearing is gone. You experience only the movements you have to make to do the route. Block out any messages from your brain describing how that last move felt. You are focused on the next move, and you don't hear messages from within. You are on automatic pilot.

This is a skill that is particularly effective when you are working very close to or at your limit. For some people, this skill comes naturally, and they naturally use this on routes. If you haven't experienced this before, try it initially on short, difficult boulder problems. Then you can eventually develop it for long problems and routes, and finally apply it on things that are well within your ability.

Confine your focus to the execution of the movement.

MENTAL TRICK 12   **SELF-AFFIRMATION**

The level of self-confidence you experience is related to a number of issues stemming back to your development as an infant and child. No two individuals ever experience the exact same things because so much of what we experience is dependent upon our perception of it. Regardless of how you feel about yourself and your climbing performance, the following activity can improve your perspective.

In a journal, write three thoughts that include what you want to accomplish in a positive and present state. You may have a goal, for example, to free a route in Yosemite. Don't write the affirmation as a goal: "I will free *The Salathe* by August 2001." Instead, write the affirmation this way: "I can free *The Salathe*." If you find this difficult, select an easier goal—"I can climb 5.12+" or "I can do five laps on 5.11." As you continue to train or climb that day, rehearse this thought in your mind, and recognize the pleasant feelings this brings out for you. Try to maintain this feeling of confidence as you approach and try each route. Practice this activity consistently, and with time, you will see a change in your self-confidence.

Positive statements lead to realized goals.

Longtime Boulder climber Jim Collins looked at the route *Genesis* (5.12d) in Eldorado Canyon in 1978. He realized that although he felt *Genesis* was a route that pushed the best climbers of the time, in ten years it would be a route that climbers on-sighted. Jim felt he was in the height of the bell-curve distribution of climbers. There were climbers better than he was, and climbers worse than himself. However, the curve over grades would shift. By 1989, the standard level for beginners would shift toward the average level of climbers in 1978. Similarly, the standard for the elite climbers would shift forward to routes not yet established in 1978. Given this probable outcome, Jim realized that he would be able to do *Genesis* in 1989. He went to a store the next day and bought a date book. He went through the book and changed the year to read 1989. Then he trained specifically for that route. The following year, he went to *Genesis* and successfully did the first ascent. It was 1979, although theoretically it was "1989." Jim simply followed the progress goals that would lead to his performance goal. And he shortened the time-line from ten years to one.

PERFECTIONISM

No one is perfect, and yet often we expect perfection of ourselves. The need to be perfect or to perfect your performance holds you back and makes the experience, the process, less fun. Being perfect is impossible; thus, it is an unreasonable expectation. Failure, which often occurs with unreasonable expectations, leads to a negative attitude and further failure. This becomes a vicious cycle, which can also lead to lower self-confidence, and on and on it goes—until no gratification is gained and you stop climbing. Although this may seem rather dramatic, you may be surprised at how many participants are expecting perfection of themselves. The following signs can tip you off to a perfectionist, perhaps even the perfectionist tendency in yourself. A perfectionist will constantly dwell on the failing rather than the process. In some ways, you may measure your success by the opinion of others, but allowing others' opinions to matter is a sign of a desire to be perfect. The search for perfectionism can lead only to failure, self-doubt, indecision, and tunnel vision.

MENTAL TRICK 13	**CLIMB ON INSTINCT**

During your training time, learn to apply new things about climbing—dropknees, back steps, and pivots. On your performance days, climb on instinct. Analyze on the ground. Once on the route, do the moves until you fall. **Commit to the moves. Trust your instinct.**

REMEMBERING THE PROCESS

MENTAL TRICK 14	**CLIMB FOR THE PROCESS**

If you think you exhibit traits of perfectionism, then try to recall how you approached climbing when you first started. You went out with some friends, and because everything was so new, there were no real expectations. You could do the hardest move, but couldn't do the easiest one on the route, and it was the exact opposite on the next. There was no consistency in what you did or didn't do. But you kept going back and climbing again. You enjoyed the process, the part of climbing that was fun. For some, as you excel, you begin to forget the process and to develop expectations and goals. Your attitude has become less flexible—you can no longer laugh if you fall on 5.9. You have lost the purpose of climbing.

Reconnecting with the process is crucial to maintaining the pure enjoyment of climbing. The first step is to release your expectations. Let go of how you should perform. If you find this step difficult and you still get frustrated when you fall off something at your on-sight level, get on something ridiculously over your head. As you fall all over this route, laugh at yourself and try to get in touch with what it felt like when you had just started and everything was way too hard, but it was fun.

The keys to curing yourself of perfectionism are to set flexible goals, to recognize the need for ups and downs on the road to improvement, and to simply enjoy the process.

MENTAL TRICK 15	**VISUALIZE THE EXPERIENCE**

In a state of relaxation, remember a particular climb, re-creating the experience in your mind. Try to remember as many things about the experience as possible—the sounds, smells, background noise, the feeling of a good performance. You want to re-create as closely as possible this positive experience. The more details you can remember, the closer the experience will be to the real thing. Recognize your ability to bring forth these feelings and continue to practice it.

Re-create a positive climbing experience.

MENTAL TRICK 16	**DIRECT YOUR FOCUS**

Select a route you would like to redpoint. Close your eyes and repeat the sequence of hands, body positions, and foot moves throughout the route. Spend five minutes on this process. When you climb the route, stay focused on the holds you are climbing on. Don't stray to the anchors until you have them in your hands.

Don't climb a route; climb each move of the route.

SLUMPS

Slumps can happen to every athlete. Everyone experiences a slump of some form or another, be it in our work, our relationships, or our lives in general. You will not know how long it will last, but the more you stress about the slump and fight it, the longer it will exist. A slump can be described as a mountain. It will determine when you can overcome it. You are powerless to fight it, so you must instead go with it, allowing yourself to appreciate what you can accomplish.

MENTAL TRICK 17   **YIELD TO THE PROCESS**

The first thing to do when you experience a slump is to take a little break from climbing. Continue to do something to stay active. A lack of activity can lead you only to depression. When you feel you've rested enough—which shouldn't be longer than a month—it's time to make a comeback. It is crucial to your mental health to write or state out loud that you can expect the first few weeks of climbing to be difficult, almost painful. You will have lower endurance, your power may be down, and your recovery will be atrocious. The silver lining is that you can expect to technically climb well to compensate for your physical limitations, once you get the first-week shakes out of your system.

Laugh at yourself, making it a point to find your performance or some aspect of your performance amusing. You can laugh at your one good performance compared to your five poor attempts. Recognize that within two weeks, you will feel strong again. This doesn't mean you are out of your slump! Your relaxed state must continue for as long as the slump chooses to continue. If you find climbing frustrating, pick a different, new sport—such as surfing or skateboarding—and become a novice. Make the silly mistakes everyone makes when trying something new. Get beat up by waves or scrape up your knees. Laugh at yourself, but definitely enjoy yourself. The slump will eventually peter out.

You cannot force the end of a slump—just wait it out.

BURNOUT

There are countless climbers who have been climbing consistently without a break, besides Christmas and maybe the occasional wedding out of town. You are in the gym as soon as the season starts to end, and you head out to the cliffs at the first signs of good conditions. Your reward for this may include lost relationships, failing grades, or inattention to your job.

Burnout can easily happen to you when climbing becomes more like work, all-consuming and less recreational. Maybe your focus was on getting to Nationals or being able to climb your first 5.12. The irony is that because it became work, it also became less fun. When that happens, your performance will suffer. It can happen slowly, without the realization that now you rarely climb for fun, but for accomplishment instead.

Preventing Burnout

Rather than mental tricks to prevent burnout, the following are ideas to prevent it. They often involve an actual change in environment or approach, not really mental changes. To cure yourself of burnout, reread the section on slumps.

If it becomes too much work to enjoy climbing with certain people or in certain areas, the best thing to do is leave. More and more climbers are making it a policy to climb only with those people who continue to be supportive and positive about climbing. Some climbers can be very intense about their performance, and their ups and downs will have an effect on you. If you find yourself with someone who can create negativity for you, walk away and climb elsewhere.

Climb for yourself. Regardless of how close to your goals or to the top of the pack of elite climbers you get, always climb a route because you like it. Always compete because you enjoy competition. Never do anything that interferes with the enjoyment of climbing for you.

Have things in your life other than climbing. Appreciate time with friends who climb recreationally or not at all. Get involved in other outdoor activities such as boating or fishing. Identify birds or flowers; take pictures; do something that can separate you from the sport.

Travel to new and exciting climbing areas, and don't just climb. Taking time to learn about a culture and a different place can be more like a vacation, and you get to climb, too.

If time restraints are keeping you out of the climbing scene and you feel that your performance is waning, pick your favorite climbing partner and get into the gym. Nothing is more important than your health—that's your excuse. You get in that one day and walk away with a big smile and realize how much fun you just had. That will jump-start you out of your tumble toward burnout.

ANGER

MENTAL TRICK 18	CENTER YOUR EMOTIONS

If you have a difficult time with frustration and/or anger, try the following. Step off a route or problem and say to yourself "STOP." Now count to five, taking deep breaths. Relax a little, take five more breaths, then relax more. Leave the area of the route or problem, drink some water, and eat a little food. Write in your journal what you would like to accomplish in the climbing session. THIS SHOULD NOT BE A PERFORMANCE-RELATED GOAL! You may want to try a problem a certain number of times or try to climb a hard redpoint twice in a row. How much you fall is not counted! It is the fact that you are trying that matters.

Return to your climbing session with a smile and a new approach to your workout. If you get frustrated again, say "STOP." Repeat the breathing, then recognize something positive about your performance. Recognize something you need to work on, say what it is out loud, and laugh or smile as you say it. Be happy to identify something you can work on improving.

Control your anger—do not let it control you.

INJURIES

Injuries are just about everyone's worst nightmare. There is only one thing worse than being injured, and that is having to live with someone who is injured. But most climbers will eventually experience some form of an injury that will prevent them from climbing for a period of time. Again, as with slumps, you can't force it. The most frustrating part is feeling that you have no control over the situation—and in many respects, you don't. Your body will heal in its own good time. If your injury is related to your sport, it can tell you something about your training, if you listen. An injury can tell you how you need to change what you are doing. You may need to work opposing-muscle groups, focus on developing better muscular balance, or work on flexibility, or maybe it's just time to let your body rest from a buildup of fatigue.

INJURY MANAGEMENT

The following are steps to help you recover mentally from an injury. This is not the part most people focus on, but it is just as important as the actual physical healing. Without it, you won't be 100 percent again.

MENTAL TRICK 19   **SQUELCH THE PANIC**
                        AND TAKE CONTROL

Most injuries come as a surprise. *Do not panic!* An injury very rarely means that you'll never climb again. It is usually just a matter of how long before you're pulling tough again. Step two is taking control. After you recognize you are injured, start making plans for the time you will be away from climbing. Try some other sport that you have always wanted to experiment with; visit friends and family; go to places you have never been. To limit the reminders and lower the temptation it is best to travel to a place without climbing opportunities. You can focus on your career or, depending on the injury, your cardiovascular fitness. Do things that you enjoy and that make you laugh. Spend time with people who make this happen as well. Maintaining and improving your general health is something you can do when you are injured. Catch up on sleep. Eat healthy food and lots of it. Your body will be drawing on its resources to assist in recovery. You can also talk to other people who have experienced a similar setback. Listen to their experience, share your own experience, and affirm to yourself that you will recover.

As your injury improves, slowly spend more time on your rehabilitation activities. Make a plan for your recovery and reentry into climbing, tempering your initial climbing sessions and gradually building up to where you left off. Learn from this experience how to listen to your body. What were the signs before the injury? How were you performing? Were you training too much? Warming up enough? Warming down? Did you try a move too many times? Did you muscle through a move? Answering these questions can help you avoid future injuries.

Learn why an injury occurred, and take steps to prevent reoccurrence.

MENTAL TRICK 20   DEEP BREATHING

This activity can be a beneficial first step to any of the above-described exercises. Breathing through your nostrils, inhale slowly, pushing your abdomen out as far as possible. When you reach your extent, straighten your back and lift your head, taking in more oxygen. Hold the breath for five seconds. Exhale fully through your nostrils. Repeat this process five times, thinking about filling your chest, abdomen, and back. As you reach a relaxed state, focus on the vision in your mind, a soothing vision of something. Practice regularly prior to exercise, during the course of exercise, and after activity.

As with anything challenging in life, moving outside your comfort zone provides you with the opportunity to improve. Sustaining a healthy balance between having fun and working on emotional issues is very important. Mental training tricks can be overwhelming if your life is full of challenges in other areas. Take it all in stride. You won't get over your fear tomorrow. But in going one move higher, you've begun the process.

Chapter 10

INJURY PREVENTION

I njuries will get you nowhere fast. There are very practical approaches to assessing your injury potential, preventing injuries, and coping with chronic problems. In every sport, athletes must cope with injuries. The people who continue to excel after an injury are those who are aggressive in rehabilitation and prevention.

CLIMBING INJURIES

My husband, Nick, on a fantastic route called *Zulu*, had to do some pretty powerful moves, for him, at the start. One move involved a left-hand two-finger crimper undercling, with a high right foot and lower left foot. The push from the foot would give him enough purchase in the undercling so that he could reach with the right hand. He repeatedly tried this move, trying to figure out the nuances and improve his performance. Unfortunately, he didn't listen to his finger. He said it felt a little sore, but tried the move again anyway. We spent the next four weeks recovering while visiting family.

Climbing has progressed from recreational status to a sport with a need for coaches and trainers. Climbers who have "trained" to improve their performance have answered that need—somewhat. Unfortunately, not all climbing "coaches" and "trainers" have experience helping someone prevent injuries. This means that climbing has new safety issues. Not safety related to belay skills, to falling, or to smashing into things, but safety from the perspective of training-related injuries.

The most prevalent injuries associated with climbing involve the upper limbs—the shoulders, arms, or hands. This makes sense, considering the load-bearing these body parts are expected to do, and considering that these parts are usually not exercised to this same degree in other mainstream activities or sports as they are in climbing. It is therefore important that the climber has a good balance of muscle development in the forearms, upper arms, and shoulders.

TYPES OF INJURIES

Injuries can be classified into one of two groups: overuse (chronic) injuries or trauma (acute) injuries. The difference is in the process of sustaining the injury. A trauma injury occurs suddenly from a force applied that is too great to sustain the muscle or

tendon. For example, dislocation of the shoulder can occur suddenly from a foot slipping off a hold and the body weight falling onto the shoulder with a great enough force to cause the humerus bone (the upper arm) to move out of its position in the shoulder girdle. Bone dislocation can result in torn ligaments or tendons of muscles surrounding the joint.

An overuse injury is caused by continual use of muscle or tendon tissue that results in little strains that eventually add up to a larger problem. Impingement is a good example of an overuse injury, in which the head of a tendon passes through a canal of bone in the shoulder area. If the muscle and tendon are worked continuously, the muscle can develop to the extent that it takes up more of the space within the canal. You experience a sharp pain when you raise your arm over your head. The tendon is pinched within the small space of canal during this motion. This impingement will not suddenly appear; it is a problem that develops with time. This is one example of an overuse injury, but there are many others. Impingement is described in detail in the book *The 7-Minute Rotator Cuff Solution.*

COMMON INJURIES AND THEIR CLASSIFICATION

Most climbing-related injuries are associated with tendons as opposed to ligaments or muscles. The muscle fibers change in density and material toward their origin and insertions. This connective tissue is called the tendon, and it is this part of the muscle that is attached to bone. Tendons are either at the origin or insertion of a muscle. The origin is the starting point, and the insertion is on the other side of a joint. It is this setup that allows for flexion and extension of body parts. Ligaments are made up of connective tissue as well, and like tendons, they assist in the stability of the joint, but they are the links between bones.

Shoulder Injuries

Of the numerous upper-limb injuries associated with climbing, probably the most common is to the rotator cuff. The rotator cuff is a band of tendons from four different small and deep muscles that surround the humerus and hold the head of the bone in the shoulder joint when the arm is elevated above ninety degrees. Because climbing inherently works the joint with the arm raised above ninety degrees, this cuff is required to sustain a great deal of force continuously. This can lead to overuse injuries, though the rotator cuff often suffers by the shock loading of the arm in a raised and rotated fashion.

Similar in symptom, though different in function, is impingement, where a tendon that runs through the acromion process (the pointy bone on the top of the shoulder joint) is pinched when the arm is elevated above ninety degrees. Impingement can be brought on by an increase in muscle/tendon size as a result of increased use and/or by the imbalance of frontal muscle to back muscle around the shoulder joint.

Some climbers have complained of a dislocation of one head of the biceps tendons. This particular tendon sits in a groove at the head of the humerus and slides with flexion of the biceps. In the case where the arm is elevated and rotated, the tendon has been known to slide out of the groove and cause pain and weakness.

Elbow Injuries

Many climbers complain of elbow tendonitis, which is a very broad term for pain at the elbow that may be felt on the inside or the outside of the arm. Pain on the outside of the forearm can be linked to injury to the tendon insertion of the triceps muscle or to the forearm extensors. Many times in climbing, the biceps gets a lot of work and grows to meet the demand; however, the triceps can be neglected and then suffer strain under a powerful contraction of the biceps. As the biceps contracts, the triceps must extend. During powerful contractions, a weaker opposing muscle may not withstand the sudden elongation. This can result in tendon injury.

When the pain is felt on the inside of the upper portion of the forearm, it may be related to the muscle that rotates the forearm and wrist. This muscle is called the brachioradialis. You may experience pain during a stressed rotation of the wrist or during resistance to flexion of the fingers. These symptoms are similar to the signs of a tight fascia, or sheath over the muscle. To differentiate between the two, a tendon issue or the sheath, try to locate a specific point of pain. If there is general pain that seems inherent to the area, rather than a point specific pain, it is more likely a fascia strain. Tendon pain will be point specific in most instances.

Finger Injuries

S. R. Bollen, in his articles concerning climbing-related injuries (1990 and 1988), notes that climbers experience a greater incidence of hand injuries than any other type of injury. Bollen has also managed to narrow down the most common complaint among climbers—a ruptured pulley. The fingers have tendon attachments that occur along the inside of the hand. The pulleys are strips of tissue that hold the tendon next to the bone (as sort of a backup) to cause the bone to flex at the knuckle joints as the forearm muscles shorten. Because the tendon strains against the pulley during this flexion, and because the tendons in the hand are generally quite strong from our climbing activities, the pulley is the weaker link and often fails before the tendon.

Another common finger injury involves the tendons, and can include injury from the finger up through the hand and into the forearm. Generally this pain is related to open-handed forces, and can be the symptom of an actual tear or strain of the tendon. If there is a lack of elasticity in the tendon, the application of force will cause the tendon to strain. This can usually be described as a tightness or burning pain. If you actually tear the tendon, a very sharp pain would be experienced.

Other injuries occur, but not as frequently as those of the upper limbs. Most of the overuse injuries affecting the upper limbs can be avoided if the appropriate rest is taken, if you listen to the signals from your muscles and joints, and if you stretch. Avoiding acute injuries is more difficult, but not impossible.

AVOIDING INJURIES

Climbing has been a rather unorganized sport in terms of technique and injury prevention. Most gyms focus on teaching you the safety skills required to pass a belay test, but few, if any, focus on a muscle-development approach that would prevent muscle imbalances, overuse, and acute injuries. Here are some ideas that may help you.

Warming Up Well

If you are one of the many who neglect to warm up, you can expect to eventually experience an injury. This includes those who consider a good warm-up to be one or two routes. So what is a good warm-up? A warm-up involves progressing from an easy level to a more difficult level of climbing. An effective warm-up prevents you from getting flash pumped, but increases the blood flow and oxygen supply to the muscles. When you are ready to try your hardest, the muscles are ready for the intensity of work you plan to attempt. This means you have to warm up to this level of difficulty you are planning to try. For example, if you are going to do V5 boulder problems, you need to warm up to V3 and V4 moves. Likewise, if you are going to do a difficult crux on a route, you need to warm up your power to that level of difficulty.

Rest Between Climbing Days

As noted in *Performance Rock Climbing,* if not enough rest, or not enough appropriate rest, is taken between climbing days, your chances of getting injured are exponentially higher. The pattern of rest is outlined in chapters 6 and 7. However, this pattern will vary for each individual, depending on your level of recovery. Similarly, training will allow you to rest less and climb more as your recovery improves. Err on the side of caution until you have a good understanding of how quickly you recover. Begin with forty-eight hours between power-training sessions and assess whether you were able to perform better. Slowly experiment with less rest.

For power-endurance days of a high intensity, begin with forty-eight hours and climb hard. Rest overnight or one day and see if you can still perform at the same level. If you can, then you could decrease the rest time. If not, continue to rest twenty-four hours until your performance on your second day on improves.

With lower-intensity workouts, endurance, and stamina, you can get by with twelve hours' rest. However, few people can effectively perform if they climb more than two days in a row, assuming that you actually climb to a level of fatigue on each climbing day. If your sessions are short and not greatly tiring, you may be able to maintain a similar level of intensity for a few days in a row. This is not the most effective means of improving performance quickly, unless your goal is to spend a few days on a big wall.

During Climbing Sessions

The training practices outlined in chapter 5 describe the amount of rest to take between routes or attempts. However, this is only a guide. If you find that your performance is continually diminished to the point that you don't feel like you can get anything done, increase the rest between tries by five to ten minutes.

Your goal is to be able to minimize the rest between attempts and still see improved performance. Studies indicate that fit climbers, on-sighting at the 5.12– level, have reached the highest level of recovery from fatigue they can expect in twenty minutes' rest (Watts, 1995). Because these climbers were required to continuously climb at the 5.12– level until failure, the level of fitness and recovery does not apply to everyone. Therefore, attempt to judge your stamina level and recovery, and use the time for you to recover as a guide to how much rest to take between routes.

Warming Down

Warming down effectively can greatly improve your recovery, leaving you with less muscle stiffness and aches. Warming down does not mean doing a route that you barely get pumped on, or falling off a route at the end of the day. It means flushing out the elements that constitute fatigue in your muscles. This means climbing at such a low level that it may be difficult for you to find a route easy enough. If you work on 5.12's, a warm-down route may be 5.7. If you climb 5.9, a warm-down may mean using elastic tubing or 1-pound weights to work out toxins in your muscles. The best guide is to warm down on a route that is two to three grades below where you begin to warm up. If you warm up on 5.9, then warm down on 5.6. If you start on 5.11–, then warm down on 5.8.

If you find that time restraints or route availability make it difficult or next to impossible to warm down, you are not off the hook. You can get on a rowing machine with the lowest resistance possible and spin through the motion. If a rowing machine is not available, use elastic tubing and do repetitions of low-resistance pull-downs, biceps curls, deltoid pulls, and female-style push-ups. If you are still complaining about the time required, then sit in a hot tub or hot bath for ten to fifteen minutes and do some stretching exercises when you get out. For examples of effective stretches, refer to the section on stretching, later in this chapter. Note that stretching can also improve technique and the possibilities of movement.

An effective warm-down and lack of muscle soreness does not mean that you don't need to rest. You should continue to take the appropriate amount of rest between climbing sessions even if you do not necessarily feel sore. Flushing lactic acid out of the muscles will reduce muscle soreness, but lactic acid does promote muscle growth and acts as a gauge to your level of fatigue.

Avoid Working Moves Continuously

Overuse injuries are generally the result of muscle imbalances or repetitive movements. This happens when working the same moves over and over again on a project. The easiest and safest way to avoid this problem is to avoid reworking moves continually and to be certain to rest enough. If you still want to figure out the body tension or positioning, then replicate the moves using jugs for the hands, but focusing on slow, static motion.

STRETCHING

An important consideration in avoiding acute and overuse injuries involves stretching. Although you groan, stretching allows the muscle to work in a more elastic fashion. If you think of the muscle tissue as having elasticity, you can visualize how it elongates when stretched and how it shortens during contraction. Now think of it as a rubber band. With time and little use, the muscle becomes less and less elastic. Unfortunately, with a lot of use, it also becomes less elastic. When the muscle becomes less elastic, or more like an old rubber band, it tears more easily when you try to extend it. It is important to note that stretching is also effective in preventing trauma injuries because the less tension over the muscle fibers, the less likely it is to sustain injury. Plus, the more a muscle can elongate, the more it can also shorten, giving more force in a contraction (this means you are stronger). More muscle strength helps prevent strain and injury.

The number of stretching books and sources on the market is mind-boggling. What follows is a relatively comprehensive guide derived from various sources, including *Climbing* and *Rock & Ice*, occupational therapists, massage therapists, gymnasts, and Pilates instructors. I suggest you attempt to practice the following stretches before and after a climbing session.

STRETCH 1	NECK ROLLS

Standing with arms straight at your sides, begin with your chin on your chest. Slowly and in a controlled fashion, roll your head in toward your left shoulder. Continue the rolling action, tilting your head backward and around to the right shoulder. Repeat this motion seven to ten times and then switch directions.

STRETCH 2	SHOULDER SHRUGS

Standing straight, with arms at your sides, lift your shoulders upward to your ear level in a slow and controlled manner, and slowly release. Do ten repetitions.

STRETCH 3   TRICEPS STRETCH

Standing upright, raise your right arm with elbow extended directly up over your head. Allow the elbow to relax and the hand to fall behind your head, as seen in the picture. Using your left hand, gently push the elbow backward behind the head. You will experience a pull through the back of the upper arm.

STRETCH 4   BICEPS STRETCH

Standing near a corner of a wall or window frame, place your arm directly out to your side, pushing against the corner or frame as shown in the picture. Rotate your body away from the edge, allowing your arm to move farther behind you as you turn. There will be a stretch through the front part of the upper arm.

STRETCH 5   FOREARM FLEXOR STRETCH

With arm outstretched in front of your body and parallel to the floor, use your opposite hand to grasp the fingers and bend the hand backward over the upper portion of the lower arm. Refer to the picture. The stretch will be experienced in the belly or lower portion of the forearm. You may experience a greater stretch at the wrist or elbow, depending on the tension within your muscle.

STRETCH 6   FOREARM EXTENSION STRETCH

Reversal of the stretch can be performed to stretch the extensor muscles of the hand. Allow the wrist to relax and the hand to drop toward the ground. Using the other hand, pull the hand toward the body and feel a stretch across the top part of the lower arm.

STRETCH 7	RHOMBOID STRETCH (Child's Pose)

The experience in this stretch is very subtle and requires deep breathing into the back for full effect. In a kneeling position, bend your upper body over your thighs and reach outward with your arms as demonstrated in the photo. Allow your chest to sag into the legs and begin the deep abdominal breathing. You may feel a subtle  pull behind your scapulae (the triangle-shaped bones in the upper back). Continue to relax and breathe for twenty to thirty seconds.

STRETCH 8	MIDDLE-BACK STRETCH

Lying on your back on a firm mat with arms and legs outstretched, lift the left leg, allowing the knee to bend at ninety degrees. When the upper leg is pointing toward the ceiling, slowly cross the leg over the body to the right. Focus on keeping the left shoulder on the ground and moving the left knee as close to the ground as possible. Doing this stretch  without the assistance of your right hand enhances your active flexibility. Using the right hand to push downward on the left knee during the stretch will increase passive flexibility.

Both are effective in increasing your range of motion through the lower back. Hold this stretch for approximately twenty to thirty seconds and repeat for the opposite leg. Repeat this stretch on both sides twice for best results. Return to the starting position when finished.

STRETCH 9   BACK STRETCH

From this relaxed starting position, bring your knees up, keeping the feet planted on the mat about hip-width apart. Round your upper body upward and grasp your shins with your hands. Allow your feet to lift from the floor and balance on your tailbone. From this position, round out your stomach area by imagining a ball fitting in there and giving it shape. Pull your belly button inward toward your spine. Allow your body to roll backward, holding this position, and then return to the upward position, rolling forward, like a ball. This will take a few tries to get the hang of it. The better you maintain the roundness of your back, the easier the stretch will be. If you find this nearly impossible, place a ball (a basketball or volleyball; a medicine ball works really well) in between your upper legs and stomach. Roll backward and forward ten to twenty times. You may not feel any stretch at all, but after the exercise, you will notice looseness in the middle of your back.

STRETCH 10   HIP ROTATIONS

Standing with feet planted shoulder-width apart, and hands on your hips, rotate your hips in a circular motion clockwise and counterclockwise. Try to keep the upper body as stationary as possible. Do approximately fifteen to twenty rotations in each direction.

STRETCH 11	SIT AND REACH

Sitting on the mat with legs out in front of you, reach with your fingertips forward to your toes. Do not lock your knees during this stretch by attempting to keep them straight as you feel the hamstring stretch. Hold the stretch for twenty seconds, relaxing into it with deep breaths.

STRETCH 12	LEG-ABDUCTOR STRETCH

Sitting with the left leg out in front of your body, bring the right leg up with a bent knee and hip flexion. Cross the right foot over the left leg at the knee. If you have difficulty crossing your knee, straighten your left leg. With the left elbow, rotate your upper body away from the legs, toward the right, and push the elbow in the other direction, to-

ward the left. You may experience the stretch through the upper back toward the shoulder or in the hip. Hold this position for twenty to thirty seconds and repeat on the opposite side.

STRETCH 13	LEG ROTATIONS

Begin by lying on your back with legs extended outward. If you experience lower-back discomfort, you can bend your knees and place your feet flat on the floor. Extend one leg and lift the leg upward as far as possible. You want to maintain your behind and opposite leg on the floor. You should feel a stretch in the back of the raised leg. Now lower the leg outward to the side of your body, as close to the floor as possible. Again you want to maintain your back on the floor. Once the leg has lowered as far as possible, rotate it back to the starting position.

Repeat this on both sides for four rotations. Then complete a second set. Remember to maintain your pressure into the floor with your back during the action.

STRETCH 14 DELTOID STRETCH

Standing up straight or kneeling with your back straight, lay your left arm over your right in front of your body. Bend your right arm at the elbow and grasp your upper arm in the triceps region. Gently pull the arm away from the shoulder. Repeat for the opposite arm, holding the stretch for approximately fifteen to twenty seconds.

STRETCH 15 BUTTERFLY STRETCH

Begin this stretch by sitting on the floor with your legs in front of you. Bend your knees and bring your feet together so the soles are touching. You now pull your feet in toward your groin until your heels are approximately 6 to 10 inches from the groin. Maintaining a straight posture, slowly lean forward, lowering your chest toward your feet. You should begin to feel a pull in the front of your groin. If you feel a stretch in the hips, your feet are too far away from the body. When you are lowered to a position of mild to moderate stretch, hold the stretch for fifteen to twenty seconds.

STRETCH 16   BUTTERFLY ADAPTATION

Begin as described above, except that this time the feet remain farther from the body, about 10 to 15 inches away from the groin. As you execute the stretch, you should feel the stretch through the sides of your behind. This loosens the hip rotators, allowing for better movement in the upper-leg rotation.

STRETCH 17   UPPER-HAMSTRING STRETCH

Begin this stretch with the left leg in front of the body and the right leg behind the body as if you were trying to do the splits. Bend the left knee and bring the foot in toward the body. Keep the right leg extended behind you during the stretch. As you allow your weight to sink into the stretch, you will feel a pull in your

upper hamstring and behind. You may also experience a stretch through the groin region as you hold this position. Hold the stretch for about fifteen to twenty seconds and then repeat on the right leg.

This is merely a guideline to get you started. There are numerous other stretches that would be helpful in maintaining range of motion and opposing-muscle strength. For more ideas, you can investigate Pilates or yoga.

OPPOSING-MUSCLE AND DEEP-MUSCLE WORK

Many people get very wrapped up in their chosen sport and focus on getting stronger and fitter. Numerous climbers spend a great deal of time working on their grip strength or back strength, trying to do pull-ups with added weight or lat pull-downs. Unfortunately, a much-neglected area is the opposing-muscle groups. Why do you want strong pecs (chest muscles) or deltoids (top of the shoulder muscles) on a climber? Opposing-muscle groups help in sustaining a healthy balance in strength, flexibility, and stability around the joint. If the opposing or opposite muscle is strong, it is less likely to be strained during a powerful contraction of the acting muscle. For example, when the biceps shortens—and it does when you lock off holds—then the triceps must elongate because it is attached on the lower side of the elbow joint. If the lock-off is performed explosively, then the triceps must respond with the same speed. If it hasn't been trained or if the triceps tendons haven't been worked with low weights and high repetitions of extension, then the triceps are in peril of tearing with such a sudden and explosive force.

In addition to attempting to maintain good muscle balance, the climber can consider getting involved in muscle work targeting the deeper muscles. Climbers have a tendency to rely on the larger-muscle groups to do the work. The latissimus dorsi muscle is called on to pull that hold down to the chest level, and the leg flexors and abdominal muscles are used to bring the foot to a high foothold. However, there are smaller muscles under the layers of the latissimus that are required to hold the head of the humerus, the upper-arm bone, in the socket of the shoulder during the pull. If those muscles aren't strengthened, injury can result. With the high foot placement, there are muscles layered under the flexors and close to the spine that can open the flexibility in the hip and groin to assist in making the movement less strenuous.

The following exercises are designed to help strengthen or bring balance to those muscles overshadowed by your typical climbing muscles. Doing these exercises can prevent a potential injury from occurring or can help deal with a current chronic problem. If you are experiencing an injury, approach these exercises very tentatively, doing things only to the point of mild discomfort. Be patient and you will slowly notice improvement, if you allow a current strain to heal first. The weights may be increased if you notice ease with these exercises. This means no soreness of muscle after completion of the activities two days in a row.

EXERCISE 18   **GRIP EXTENSORS**

Using a 1- to 2-pound weight held in each hand, hold the arms out in front of the body with palms facing downward. Curl the hands backward and upward in an arcing motion at the wrist. This exercise can be repeated eight to ten times, then rest.

EXERCISE 19   **TRICEPS ROWS**

Holding a weight of 5 to 15 pounds, extend the arm up over the head and allow the elbow to bend and the hand to hang over your back. With support on the elbow from the opposite hand, raise the weight in an upward motion, extending the arm at the elbow. Repeat these lifts for eight to ten repetitions and then switch the weight to the other hand and repeat.

EXERCISE 20   **DIPS (Triceps)**

To complete this exercise, you may need a chair or high table. Placing your arms extended and behind you, place your hands on the chair or table and suspend your weight on your hands. You then lower your body, bending your elbows, until your hands reach midway up the torso. Then straighten the elbows and raise the body until the hands are at the hips again. Repeat eight to ten times, then rest.

EXERCISE 21   ROTATOR-CUFF STRENGTHENING

With arms at the side, bend the elbow to ninety degrees. Holding a light weight, 1 to 4 pounds, rotate the arm toward and away from the body in a slow and controlled manner. This can be repeated for ten to twenty inward and outward rotations.

EXERCISE 22   DELTOID STRENGTHENING

Extend the arms at the side and raise them to shoulder height. Holding 2- to 4-pound weights, slowly lift the arms up toward the ceiling, raising the weights directly over the head. Maintain the palms facing toward the ground and the backs of the hands coming together. This exercise can be repeated for up to fifteen raises.

EXERCISE 23   LOWER-BACK STRENGTHENING

Lying on your stomach on the firm surface of a table, have a partner hold your feet. Extend your upper body over the end of the table, with the table edge at the waist. Lower the upper body downward toward the floor, keeping your arms across your chest. Slowly raise the upper body back to a vertical position, using the lower-back muscles. Repeat this exercise fifteen to twenty-five times, then rest.

All the above exercises can be done in sets, rotating through each exercise and then returning to the first exercise and repeating the process. It is recommended that you rotate through the exercises, giving different muscle groups sufficient rest prior to reuse.

ACTIVE AND PASSIVE FLEXIBILITY

In most descriptions, you are using muscle contraction to obtain a stretch of an opposing muscle. This is referred to as active flexibility. The leg rotations mentioned previously in this chapter are a good example of active flexibility, in which you are using the flexor of the leg to lift the leg upward and stretch the hamstring.

Another form of flexibility is called passive flexibility, in which you use the force of gravity or external pressure to get the maximum stretch. The benefit of active flexibility over passive flexibility is that you are also improving muscle strength and your ability to use the increased range of motion in the stretch. An example of a passive stretch is when you do the side splits, with gravity helping you get closer and closer to the floor, extending your legs out to the side.

There is also a benefit to passive flexibility in that it can help you increase your range of motion more quickly than active flexibility. When you try to improve your flexibility in the side splits, using the floor as resistance may feel more uncomfortable, but it definitely will get you closer to the floor than trying to train your adductor muscles to do the side splits.

PROPRIOCEPTIVE NEUROMUSCULAR FEEDBACK (PNF)

Using the passive-flexibility concept, a form of stretching known as proprioceptive neuromuscular feedback (PNF) has been noted to be very effective in improving flexibility, if it is practiced consistently. This form of stretching involves muscular contraction against a resistance while in a stretched position. Using the description of stretch 13 as a reference, begin in a stretch position with your legs extended out in front and to the side of you. Reach out in front of you, between your legs. Once you have reached to your fullest extent, a partner applies resistance to the middle and upper portion of your back as your try to sit upright.

It is very important during this process to push against the resistance only in a controlled and static way, with approximately 70 to 80 percent of your maximum ability. The partner is not supposed to push you farther forward, but simply prevent you from moving to an upright position. You hold this resistance push against your partner for about ten seconds, and then you can relax as your partner moves away. This can be repeated for three or four sets of resistance stretches. You will notice, if you are doing things properly, that your range of motion quickly increases.

The mechanism at work in this activity is tricking the muscle into finding a new resting position for the muscle cell. Think of your muscle cells as a pull-up bar that goes between the door frame. Either side of the bar is spring loaded so it will fit snugly between the frame of the door and stay in position with weight on it. Your muscle cells have a "resting position," or point of extension (overlap), when the muscle is not in contraction or a stretch. In a contraction, the muscle cells shorten from this resting position, inducing change in body position and an increase in tension over the cells or bundles of cells.

The opposite happens during a stretch, where you are lengthening the muscle cells to their extent. However, for most of you, there is still an overlapping section, where you have room to increase the stretch. If you are in this extended position and then attempt to shorten the muscle by contracting it, but the muscle cannot shorten because of the resistance provided against it, the muscle finds a new "resting " position. This creates two beneficial situations. The first is that you now have a greater range of motion with the body. The second is an increase in the potential force you can create from the muscle. This is the biggest and best-kept secret about flexibility. You can improve your muscle's capacity to generate a greater force by improving its resting position.

PILATES AND ROLFING

For many of us, climbing involves the use of our larger outer muscles—the latissimus dorsi, the trapezius muscles, rhomboids, abdominal muscles, and so forth. However, underneath this structure of large exterior muscles are numerous smaller muscles. Because we rarely spend time getting to know our muscular structure, we often have no awareness of the existence of these muscles. Our bodies nonetheless are good at compensating for us and developing the required muscles to maintain our fitness in most cases. What we are missing, by not using these smaller muscles to their full potential is the opportunity for increased overall strength and recovery. Getting to know these muscles and using them in movement is a learned thing, much like infants learning to walk. It doesn't happen all at once; it takes practice and awareness.

The Pilates system is designed to assist in the development of deep-muscle work. There are numerous Pilates exercises that you can do at home with limited resources, although some exercises can involve elaborate equipment. The benefits to Pilates work is better flexibility through your body and the ability to control and incorporate deeper muscles in work. Although it takes practice to tie Pilates strength gains to climbing, if you are patient and work on it, you can get there. For information on a Pilates program near you, call 1-800-PILATES.

Rolfing, or structural integration, is another method of discovering and creating an inner balance. The theory behind the work is that with time, our bodies compensate for the physical traumas and effects of gravity. This compensation leaves us with muscle memory that creates imbalances and, in some cases, chronic discomfort. The action of structural integration is to reorganize the connective tissue, or fascia. This restructuring releases stress and encourages you to use your body more efficiently. Many Rolfers recommend Pilates as follow-up strengthening work.

Having suffered chronic muscle spasms in the left middle of my back, I was interested in trying Rolfing to see if it would make a difference. It did! In 1995, while writing a thesis and preparing to pick myself up and move to another city across the country, trying to salvage my relationship and still power-train, I overdid it and caused a muscle spasm to tear through my back on the left side. Breathing was difficult for the first few days, and anything more extreme was out of the question. Over the next four years, too much training, long bouts of computer time, and stress would cause it to go into spasm again. In the winter of 1999, I went through the ten series with the Guild for Structural Integration in Boulder, Colorado. Although I was climbing with clients as many as twenty hours per week, as well as climbing on my own and writing a book, I have not had a hint of muscle spasms since. And during the course of the work, I discovered that my ape index* had increased 2¹/4 inches. I highly recommend the work.

Avoiding High-Injury-Potential Body Positions

It can be difficult to avoid injuries, because they may result from a sudden loading or impact over a joint. However, by climbing in body positions that limit the potential for sudden force loading in an injurious stance, you can eliminate some of the potential. I'm sure you have all watched as a climbing partner has locked off a hold at his chest and is suddenly paralyzed, unable to move the other hand to the hold above. His body begins to shake, you are yelling your encouragement, and his elbow starts to rotate out behind him. We call this chicken winging, and many of us know it is a sure sign of failure—once that starts, the climber won't do the move. But this is also an injury-potential position.

*The ape index, measured in inches, expresses the relationship between a person's arm span and height. An arm span greater than one's height is termed a positive ape index and is supposedly an advantage for climbers.

HIGH-RISK BODY POSITION 1   ELBOWS OUT

Hanging onto the holds with your elbows rotating outward, known as "chicken-winging," greatly compromises the elbow and shoulder tendons.

HIGH-RISK BODY POSITION 2   HIGH GASTON

A second injury-potential position is with the arm extended over the head and the hand rotated away from the body, reaching up and back at the same time. In this position, the climber has a great potential for injury to the rotator cuff. Most therapists will recommend not reaching over your head and putting force on your hand in this position, which could be impractical advice for many climbers to follow. But the higher you place your feet and the more you can shift your hips toward the hold you are loading in this fashion, the less dangerous the position becomes.

When you climb in such a way that the arm is raised over the head and the thumb is pointed downward in a gaston position, the shoulder is placed in a highly dangerous position. As the arm

(continued)

HIGH-RISK BODY POSITION 2   HIGH GASTON *(continued)*

is raised over the head, the rotator cuff must work to maintain the head of the humerus, the upper-arm bone in the joint. When the arm is then rotated internally, as with the gaston position, the rotator cuff is under greater tension.

Dynamic Movement
Dynamic movement can be instrumental in causing acute injury, by the very nature of landing suddenly on the fingers. The campus board is a tool used by many to practice doubles, where you throw both hands upward to the next rung, feet off entirely. The landing position for this is open hands sustaining body weight, times the force of gravity on your fingers. I recall being in a gym where the route setters set numerous problems with dynos in them, because they are fun. They are fun, but they also increase the chance of injury substantially. More-static movement, where the feet maintain a percentage of the body weight, generates less force applied strictly to the fingers, and thus can eliminate injury potential.

NUTRITION AND HYDRATION
There are signs and symptoms in injury that can be linked to a lack of proper nutrition and hydration. During high-intensity work, your body continually uses previously digested nutrients for energy. This source of energy must be replenished shortly following work. Without adequate nutrients and amino acids, the building blocks of protein, the body cannot repair and regenerate tissue affected by the work.

During activity, the body also uses water within the cells to assist in contractile properties of muscle fibers and as a method of decreasing core temperature that increases in response to exercise. This water is a necessary component of osmotic balance in the cells. Without continued hydration, the body becomes less efficient in muscle contraction and neural signaling. This dehydration can result in tissue injury.

THE BOTTOM LINE IN INJURY PREVENTION
The optimum approach to avoiding or limiting your potential for injury involves practicing all of the above-mentioned ideas—stretching, strengthening, doing things in less-injurious body positions, not reworking continuously, warming up appropriately, and climbing in a more static fashion. Although these practices can go a long way toward decreasing your potential for injury, not all injuries can be avoided, so be smart.

Chapter 11

TRUTH OR CONSEQUENCES

*U*nfortunately, climbing has developed on its own recognizance, with the participants themselves defining the causes and effects in training and performance. Often, coincidence in experience has led professional climbers to believe that they understand how training works. In some instances, a climber will have hit on a truth or discovered something about himself or herself, which in many cases does not work for other people. This history of anecdotal understanding in the sport has led to numerous misconceptions.

THE FLASH PUMP

I have frequently heard, "I climb better second day on." I quickly begin to probe a little deeper into the mystery of the better performance second day on. One would think that directly following a rest, you would climb better. For most people, this is true. The usual reason for this experience of climbing better after a day of climbing is that you haven't warmed up properly on the first day. After an extended rest, you may take more pitches and at a slower rate to get a good warm-up. If you don't take the required time to warm up, you can experience a flash pump. This means that the muscles go into a very high level of oxygen debt quickly, and therefore your recovery will be slow. Once you get a flash pump, you have lost at least 20 percent of your potential. You will not get it back until you have had, in most cases, twenty-four or more hours of rest.

In order to avoid a flash pump, the best thing to do is to let go if you start to feel really pumped on something that should be relatively easy for you. The other thing that you could do, if letting go goes against all that is natural for you, is to work on your recovery and try to improve it to a level where you increase what you can regain after a pump. Recovery exercises are outlined in chapter 5. It would also be prudent to consider warming up more gradually in the future.

WEIGHT LIFTING

Many elite climbers claim that lifting weights is an effective means of preventing injury and gaining strength, as it has been described in detail in chapter 10. This is true in many situations. Lifting weights to strengthen opposing-muscle groups is effective in preventing injury. Weights can also improve muscle strength. However, time spent lifting weights *will not necessarily* translate to improved climbing performance because it does not allow for improved technical skill. In the case where you first come to the sport of climbing and have never done anything like it, besides learning some basic movement skills, a little weight training could be beneficial in getting you to a point where you could stay on the wall longer and practice more skills.

Or if you live in the same kind of situation I did when I started climbing, weight lifting could be the only activity you can do during the off-season. If there is no wall, something is better than nothing to maintain your climbing strength and fitness.

If, however, you have only four hours a week to exercise, and you have some level of climbing fitness, your time would be better spent climbing than weight lifting to see improved performance. Lifting weights will not teach you how to drop-knee, where to do it, or the subtlety of the movement.

On the other hand, if you want to be a world-class climber and have committed yourself to a full-time training regime, weight lifting could definitely benefit you. With the hours of climbing you will be doing, your skin will be a problem, and there will be the issue of opposing-muscle-group strength and injury prevention. In this scenario, weight lifting is an effective tool in improving your overall success.

When to weight train relative to your climbing schedule becomes the next issue of importance. If you prefer to see your best performance in your climbing, then climb when you have had the most rest, and weight lift at the end of your climbing session or later that day. It is best to try to do both in the same day until you can build up your recovery to a point where weight training doesn't affect your climbing performance if you have only twelve hours' rest.

CROSS-TRAINING

There is a lot of buzzing about out there concerning cross-training and VO_2 max. Your VO_2 max refers to the maximum amount of oxygen that your lungs can hold. Obviously, the greater the VO_2 max, the better your ability to prevent oxygen debt during exercise. For many years, sport scientists believed that improvement of the VO_2 max resulted from endurance work. Now, however, studies show that your VO_2 max can be increased just about as quickly with anaerobic training, such as redpointing.

There are some climbers who do run or bike to better their VO_2 max, and who swear it makes a difference in their climbing. I would question whether it is truly improving their climbing performance to the extent that they believe. A VO_2-max test must be conducted on a person while he or she executes a skill to failure. Measurements of expired air are taken during the test, and the analysis of this expired air allows a technician to calculate the max VO_2 for that person. The results of this test will vary depending on the muscle groups used in the test. A rowing-machine test may produce different results from the same person doing the test on a bike or treadmill. Relative to climbing, a rowing machine may give a more accurate result because part of the VO_2-max test involves the transfer of oxygen and demand of the muscle doing the work. Similar to the weight-lifting concept, certain limitations may lead you to use cross-training, specific to upper-body work, as a way to enhance climbing performance, provided you have the additional time for this exercise. If you have the time and the inclination to be the best you can be, running or biking definitely won't take away from your climbing, unless you run into a car or have some accident. If you are limited by time, stick to climbing if that is your priority. Your VO_2 max will improve either way as long as you increase intensity.

Again, as with weight training, cross-training can affect your climbing performance adversely, if it is done prior to a climbing session. You may think, "How can a 2-mile run interfere with my climbing—it's not the same muscles at all?" But it will drain your energy and you must condition yourself to a point where it doesn't. To make sure you have a better climbing session than your run, run after climbing, but preferably on the same day. This will give you your best climbing recovery before your next climbing day.

DIET

Everyone adapts somewhat to a diet that he or she is used to eating, and everyone responds differently to changes in the norm. Some people tout the benefits of a high-protein diet, while others say carbo loading is the way to go. There are also diets that describe different people as needing different allotments of food elements—carbohydrates, fats, proteins. There are books for athletes and books for dieters. It can be very overwhelming—and a lot of nonsense.

After many years of attempting to control my own diet—while food was actually controlling me—the best and easiest advice this recovered anorexic can give is to incorporate a variety of foods into your meals, allowing yourself fruits and vegetables (vitamins and minerals, carbohydrates), meat, beans (protein), and oils (fat). If you are vegetarian, I definitely suggest that you pay very close attention to combinations of foods that will ensure a substantial amount of protein. Sport climbing is not usually an endurance sport, and therefore you are continually taxing your body in the recovery of tissue and the building of new tissue. This requires amino acids, which come from sources of protein. Big wall climbing, however, is endurance-oriented and requires continual funding with carbohydrates.

Personally, I choose foods with fewer preservatives, foods that tend to be more natural. While not spending a fortune on organic food products, I do tend to use spices to make meals more interesting and to boost circulation. I also prefer to obtain carbohydrate supply from fruits and vegetables over high-starch foods such as rice, potatoes, and pasta, thus increasing the anti-oxidants in my diet.

PERFORMANCE-ENHANCING DRUGS

There are many substances on the market that can enhance your performance. These are not drugs that you pick up with a prescription, either. The list includes substances with caffeine, such as soda and coffee; some cough syrups; and aspirin or ibuprofen, which improve blood circulation. These drugs are stimulants and can increase the amount of oxygen getting to the muscles during exercise. Sounds great—but they do have their downside. Caffeine is also a diuretic, forcing more-frequent urination, and thus possible dehydration. Dehydration is a very common cause of injury to muscle or tendon tissue.

Drugs such as aspirin and ibuprofen are designed to decrease inflammation and reduce pain, but they can also lead to injury. If you don't feel the initial warning signals, you can overstrain a tendon or muscle and not even know it. It is very important to listen closely to the pain messages during climbing in order to avoid unnecessary injury. Drugs can block these messages.

Creatine has become more and more popular among the climbing population. It is a substance that your body digests from food and stores in the muscle. During high-intensity work, creatine is used as a source for energy for muscle contraction. It stands to reason that the more you store, the better your performance. Creatine, however, does cause your muscles to store more water in the cells. If you don't drink enough water, you will experience muscle cramping or, worse, strain. Drinking lots of water can prevent injury, but continued dosages of creatine will cause weight gain. Although your strength is improving during the use of creatine, the weight gain will affect your endurance on holds.

Glucosamine sulfate is another natural substance that is supposed to be effective in improving joint health. Glucosamine is an amino acid that is responsible for tissue repair. It is found in protein, particularly meat products. Climbers, particularly those who are vegetarians, report good results with this supplement.

5.12 IS SO HARD

For many people out there, 5.12 seems like a really hard level of climbing, but in reality, it's not. However, the harder you think it is, the longer it will take you to get there. The same applies to any grade you post on that pedestal. If there are climbers out there who can on-sight 5.14, how hard can it be?

One of the interesting things about the younger generation of climbers is their attitude. Kids will throw themselves at just about anything with little reservation, and that is one of the reasons why they excel. Although you can't change your age, you can change your attitude. Let go of your preconceived notions about grades and just climb!

CLIMBING TO FAILURE IS A NECESSARY PART OF IMPROVEMENT

Many climbers who take training seriously feel the need to climb until absolute failure before calling it quits for the day. In 1998, I was climbing in Rifle City Park with a couple from Canada, Sonny Trotter and his girlfriend Lisa. These two did a maximum of four routes a day—nowhere near failure. During their three-week visit, Sonny would do three 5.14a's, and Lisa successfully redpointed a 5.13a; neither of them had ever climbed those grades before. I don't cite this example as a training recommendation, but it suggests that sometimes you can get more from less.

The greater the level of fatigue in your body, the more you need to recover. As the level of fatigue decreases and strength increases, you can see better performance. However, if the fatigue has been accumulating for months, the recovery needed can be greater than the strength or fitness gains achieved, and so no improvement is evident. A continued climbing plan adding to this fatigue can lead directly to injury—not to mention, at the very least, a great deal of frustration.

When recovering from high levels of fatigue, it is important to rest your mind as well as your body. Motivation can begin to ebb when you've been pushing yourself for extended periods of time. Climbing less during a session and resting more has been the success of the Austrian National Ski Team. It may work for you.

TAPING IS A GOOD WAY TO PREVENT INJURY

Although using tape to support the joints can be effective in preventing further injury of the finger, that doesn't mean it can prevent injury. In fact, if you forget your tape one day, you could have just set yourself up to have a greater potential for injury. Your body will adapt to having the support of tape. When you neglect to tape, you have created a greater potential for harm.

In my experience, most people do not know how to tape to prevent further injury. Placing tape around your finger does nothing to prevent a torn tendon, pulley, or ligament, unless the tape has a supportive action to it. Taping effectively means knowing how the tendons, pulleys, and/or ligaments around the joint work, and how to limit the range of motion and strain on the specific connective tissue you wish to support and protect. It is best to use tape to protect torn skin and to support an already problematic joint. However, eventually you should wean yourself from the use of tape by gradually loosening the wraps.

CLIMBING IS ALL ABOUT STRENGTH

Climbing is hardly all about strength. True, many factors that can make a good climber do involve a base level of strength. But strength is a relative thing. Some people are better designed for endurance sports, while others excel in power sports, but that is hardly relevant at the 5.13 level of climbing. As previously discussed, there are short, burly climbers and long, lean types—both climbing 5.14. The beauty of the sport is that it offers a variety of types of climbs—long, technical routes and short, powerful ones. Regardless of your physique, climbing is as much about your mental tenacity and your technique as it is about your physical ability.

Having said that, climbing may soon become more about strength in combination with technique and mental stamina. The size of holds on V14 and powerful 5.14+ hedges in that direction. If you can't hang on to something really small, and if you can't pull with one arm on it, either, chances are you eventually will be stopped in your conquest of grades. But for most of us, that is down the road a ways.

GENDER DIFFERENCES

In the realm of physiology and physical stature and appearance, men and women are different. But how this affects climbing really depends on the individual and his or her goals. Men may have greater levels of testosterone and a predisposition for high levels of power, recovery, and stamina. On the other hand, women seem better able to find balance and generally are more flexible. The relativity of this takes us back to the beginning of this book and the physiology of routes. While some 5.14's—for example, *To Bolt Or Not To* in Smith Rock, Oregon—may be geared toward balance and flexibility, other routes—such as *Lung Fish* in Rifle Canyon—demand more power. While one could argue that this is not gender specific—rather, style specific—the contention here is that there are generalizations that can be made on the basis of gender. The available power and sense of balance are two of them. Women are known to have wider and a more-shallow hip structure to enable them to bear children. This different hip structure lowers a woman's center of gravity compared to that of a man. A lower center of gravity will affect the movement patterns of a climber.

On the other hand, it is known that men have higher levels of testosterone and, according to a great deal of research, a greater potential to develop power. This seems reinforced by the fact that very few women have bouldered harder than V10. It is also somewhat evident when you begin to consider the nature of the routes that women have completed at the higher grades. Are they oriented more toward power, toward finesse, or toward power endurance?

Then there is the mental aspect of the sport. Men seem able to feed on each other, challenging themselves and fellow competitors on boulder problems. Women do not generally seem to work as well in this type of competitive arena. Many of the women with whom I have climbed express the feeling that they prefer to work at a level where they have a fairly good chance at success—that is, they like to work within their comfort zone.

Examination of the socialization of men and women has shown that there are differences in how the genders act and react in different situations. Some research indicates that women in general have lower levels of self-esteem than do men. However, women also appear to be more tenacious than men are.

You may not like these generalizations, or you may even feel that these differences don't they really exist. More important is the concepts that, to improve, you need to work on your weaknesses. If you fit these generalizations, you may need to focus more time on power training. Your needs may be more in the direction of becoming more aware of your center of gravity and balance. You may need to be more tenacious or strive for a stronger belief in yourself and your abilities. In the sections on mental training and physical training, you will find activities that can assist you in working on weaknesses.

ONE OF ANYTHING IS PLENTY

It is an interesting enigma in this sport that people think that one pair of shoes or one rope or one harness fits the bill for anything they want to accomplish. This is not true. If you look into other sports—say, running—there are different shoes for track versus distance running. Or take a look at the equipment for paddling. People have different boats or surfboards for different wave and water conditions. You can climb in anything, but do you want to climb, or are you looking to meet greater challenges in the sport? If you bought this book, you most likely want to get better, and equipment is part of that.

All the different types of shoes that the shoe companies make have a different purpose. One style is designed for steep climbing, another for more-vertical rock. One shoe will be better for toeing into pockets; another will push your foot out of the pocket, but will excel at edging. The different companies usually provide different shoes to meet a variety of needs, but they also have different lasts. The last is the shape and stiffness of the shoe. Some companies design shoes for a more European foot, and others for a wider foot. Some companies deal with the issue of differences between men and women's feet.

The biggest determining factor in which shoe company you buy from will be fit. Other factors will include how stiff a shoe you need, the toe box, the heel cup, and the ease of wear. For example, slippers make good gym shoes because they are easy to take off and put on, and the footholds usually protrude from the wall. Slippers tend to be a little softer than some of the stiffer shoes, and can make your feet really tired or even be painful on edges in the outdoor environment.

Stiffer shoes are usually what employees of sport stores recommend to beginners because it is harder to wear them out. Thus, the shoe lasts longer. Unfortunately, this shoe will also cause the climber to climb with poor footwork, a hard habit to break. Usually a softer shoe enhances foot precision and awareness; thus, it can be better for learning in, even if it does wear faster.

Some—but not all—climbers have caught on to the pros and cons of different harnesses. There are harnesses that are designed to be lightweight, with minimized features and improved freedom of movement. Other harnesses are made to be worn all day for several days. They have lots of gadgets for holding a lot of gear, but they provide less freedom of movement. And there are harnesses in the middle. It doesn't hurt to have one for hard redpointing and another for working routes or belaying your partner while he or she figures out the sequence on their next project. You can definitely argue that there is no need for more than one harness, but if you are a serious climber, you will be wearing out your harness within two years; in some cases, one year. So why work a sequence on a new project for an hour, hanging in a small harness? It would be better to have a harness for belaying and working routes, especially if you plan to start training intervals and recovery or stamina, and another harness for sending. Both will give you better wear, more comfort, and better mental tenacity and motivation for long climbing sessions.

Ropes! Everybody usually has one, but have you thought about how that one rope takes abuse on top-rope sessions or work sessions of routes? Maybe you have, and that's why you choose to buy the 10.5 millimeter for durability, or maybe even an 11 millimeter. Well, the extra weight from a thicker rope will make it harder to send. Or you may experience getting short-roped when your belayer struggles to get the rope through the belay device. It may be more prudent to buy a thin rope for sending and a thicker rope for working routes and warming up. This way, your rope on redpoint is always in better condition, giving you more confidence and better handling.

SPOTTING

Confusion seems to abound in the world of spotting. I have seen some pretty bad spots—situations where the climber ended up with broken wrists or torn ligaments in his ankles. The objective in spotting a climber is to prevent the head from hitting the ground. Contrary to the popular belief that the spotter must catch the climber, the spotter's intent should involve assisting the climber in landing on his feet.

For the past few years, the Boulder Rock Club has hosted the annual "Ultimate Man Competition." The conception of this competition was the work of Pat Adams, Jimmy Redo, and Jonathan Thesenga while all three were route setters for the club. This competition is an invitational competition to the local hard men—and, more recently, women—in the Boulder area. The format includes three routes, a highball boulder problem, and a mystery event to break ties. The mystery event has in the past included logrolling or a campus-board event based on artistic impression, rather than strength.

The highball boulder problem for the 1999 event was approximately 22 feet high. Although a couple of 2-foot-thick mats were used, the spotter, Jonathan Thesenga, was instrumental in preventing injury. Competitor Nick Sagar, who flashed the problem and was told that down climbing would negate the ascent, described Jonathan's spot as "being caught." Jonathan's unique technique is very similar to that of another famous North American spotter and climber, Greg Loh. Both these spotters have the ability to literally catch the falling climber and slow the body's momentum en route to the ground.

This technique does not and will not work for everyone. If you are of smaller stature and worry about your own injury in spotting others, then use your mass to keep the climber's head from hitting the ground. Or get others around you to assist in spotting. In the gym on a busy night, it is amazing how many climbers do not get spotted even though there are many people present.

Learning to spot well is like learning to be a good belayer. While you may not appreciate always having to belay or spot, take pride in the fact that you are an instrumental part of the ascent. My husband will always be able to climb circles around me, but I know that, with me on the other end of the route, he doesn't worry about the belay or his safety. Likewise, I can pull much harder with him spotting or belaying me. While you may believe this can limit your climbing opportunities, it definitely gives you, the climber, better focus for the route.

WORKING WITH A COACH OR PERSONAL TRAINER

Due to a lack of regulatory guidelines in this sport, few people who actually offer "personal training" are qualified to do so. Even within the fitness industry, there are no guidelines for certification required to sell yourself as a personal trainer. So how do you, the prospective client, protect yourself from hiring someone who is not qualified or knowledgeable? Here are a few practical steps to take to ensure yourself of quality guidance. First, find out whether this person has any previous education in exercise physiology, kinesiology, or biomechanics. Second, ask if he or she has any certification or educational degree in the sport sciences. Although the ACE (American Council on Exercise) certification or the sports-medicine certification may not be specific to climbing physiology, it will show some training on the part of the trainer. Discuss with the trainer some of his or her previous experiences with clients. Has he or she worked with any recognizable names? What was his or her success with people who have goals similar to your own? Ask for references from other clients.

It is also important to note that, although this trainer may have a good track record in his or her own climbing, that may not translate well to improving your performance. Determine whether the trainer offers the opportunity to assess your current level of fitness, whether the trainer knows the level of fitness you will need to reach your goals, and whether he or she takes an injury-preventative approach to this process.

A trainer must be more than a cheerleader, although, for many people, motivation gained through a trainer is invaluable. A trainer should continually discuss with you the way you move, and should be constantly critiquing and fine-tuning your techniques. The task of personal training involves a continuous assessment of movement, strength, cardiovascular fitness, and flexibility. This ongoing assessment should allow the trainer to update your program every few weeks, depending on the time you spend climbing. As you evolve, so should your training practices as outlined by your trainer.

Finally, in selecting a personal trainer, you should choose the one who is trying to work himself or herself out of a job. A proficient trainer will be continually guiding you through a learning process where you will eventually have enough of an understanding of how your body works, and what you need, to become a better climber. Although you may start with a few months of ongoing work with a trainer, you will eventually be able to work on your own, going back only every six months or so for a reevaluation of your fitness, technique, and needs.

COMPARATIVE GRADE SCALE

North America	France/Spain	Bouldering
5.10b	5c+	V0
5.10c	6a+	V0
5.10d	6b	V1
5.11a	6b+	V1
5.11b	6c	V1
5.11c	6c+	V2
5.11d	7a	V2
5.12a	7a+	V3
5.12b	7b	V4
5.12c	7b+	V5
5.12d	7c	V6
5.13a	7c+	V7
5.13b	8a	V8
5.13c	8a+	V9
5.13d	8b	V10
5.14a	8b+	V11
5.14b	8c	V12
5.14c	8c+	V13
5.14d	9a	V14

Glossary

Active flexibility. The range of movement around a given joint produced through muscle work as opposed to flexibility gained with the assistance of gravitational force.

Acute injury. An injury sustained in a traumatic situation, perhaps a sudden fall. The symptoms and the injury occur all at once and without warning.

ADP (adenosine diphosphate). The by-product of the breakdown of a phosphate molecule from ATP (adenosine triphosphate). ATP contains three phosphate groups joined together. When the phosphate molecule breaks from ATP, it leaves ADP, and the released energy is used for muscle contraction. The ADP is then re-cycled for future use.

Aerobic. This means "in the presence of oxygen." Thus, aerobic work is work that is done with enough oxygen getting to the muscles during the breakdown of ATP. The significance of aerobic work is that, compared to anaerobic work, the dura-tion can be sustained for a longer period of time, while the intensity of the work may be lower.

Anaerobic. Work conducted without sufficient oxygen supplied to the muscle for the work to be aerobic. Without the presence of oxygen, the energy is gained through glycolysis or by the breakdown of creatine phosphate (phosphocreatine). The rate of energy production is faster, but more limited than, that of aerobic work. The intensity, or difficulty, of anaerobic work is much greater than that of aerobic work, but the potential duration of the activity is shorter.

Anaerobic threshold. The point where the metabolism switches from aerobic to anaerobic. This threshold is measured by the workload or oxygen consumption at the point of shift. Anaerobic capacity has been expressed as the accumulated or maximal oxygen deficit.

Anthropometric. Measurements that involve a descriptive and quantitative form of body-type analysis.

Arousal. During a state of arousal, the blood flows faster, the heart beats faster, and usually there is hormonal stimulation of the parasympathetic nervous system. This triggers the "fight-or-flight" response.

ATP (adenosine triphosphate). The source of energy for muscle contraction. When a phosphate molecule breaks from the ATP, the end result is ADP, a phosphate molecule and energy for muscle contraction.

Beta. Information concerning a route or sequence for a route that can be instrumen-tal in executing the moves on the route.

Biomechanics. The study of movement from a mechanical point of view—that is, the combined influence of the levers and joint action with the physiological element.

Bouldering. Rock climbing on short walls or boulders without a rope or harness. Unlike soloing, in bouldering, the climber will experience a ground fall and generally can work at a much higher level of difficulty due to the short nature of the problem.

Capillarization. The capillaries are the small connections between the muscle fiber and the larger arteries or veins. Capillaries will develop with increased demand for blood flow. Capillarization refers to the amount of capillaries supplying a given muscle.

Chronic injury. A reoccurring injury that continues to be a problem despite measures to heal it. For example, for many people, back problems are considered chronic and easily reoccur with strain.

Closed skill. A skill that requires focus on the routine of movement and execution of that skill. For example, a skating routine or gymnastic floor exercise is considered a closed skill. There are no variables that will change the execution or pattern of movement.

Concentric contraction. A contraction during which the muscle shortens, resulting in the movement of the two aspects around a joint.

Connective tissue. The tissue that surrounds and supports muscle and bone within the body.

Core tension. The application of strength through the abdomen and back of the body. This strength can be visible in a front lever, for example, or in a push-up in which the body remains rigid from the shoulders through the legs.

Creatine phosphate (phosphocreatine) system. An energy-supply system that provides the breaking of a phosphate molecule and the output of energy for muscle contraction. This is an anaerobic process of creating energy for work and is utilized in very-high-intensity movement.

Crimp. A small handhold that you can hold only with your fingertips and knuckles bent.

Crux. The most difficult section of a route. A power-endurance crux means doing the moves with the continued pump from all the moves before the most difficult part of the route. A powerful crux refers to very difficult movements on the route.

Dropknee. A body position used in climbing to gain height, usually on very steep terrain. For illustrations of this position, see chapter 8.

Dynamic movement. Movement that is forceful and somewhat uncontrolled. The opposite of static movement, in which the moves are highly controlled.

Eccentric contraction. A contraction of the muscle that includes lengthening of that muscle.

Efficient movement. Movement that uses the least amount of energy in the course of its execution. While this may seem like the best way of doing things, efficient movement is not always effective.

Effective movement. Movement that allows for successful execution of a skill. Effective movement may expend more energy than efficient movement does, but it has a higher factor of success.

Endomorphic. A body that is very lean, with little prominent musculature.

Endurance. Aerobic work. For example, for most people, walking is considered to be an endurance activity. There is always a generous supply of oxygen to the leg muscles during the activity, and therefore the walker does not get tired quickly.

Fascia. A sheath of material that covers the muscle bundles. This sheath is also considered to be connective tissue.

Fatigue. To the layperson, this means a level of tiredness. However, in physiological terms, fatigue is measured by levels of lactic acid in the blood.

Flag. Forcing one's leg out to the side as a counterbalance to the rotational pull on the body during transitions. For illustrations and more detail, see chapter 8.

Flash. Climbing a route for the first time and not falling, after having been given beta (information about the route). This differs from an on-sight climb, in which the climber has no previous information concerning the route.

Flexibility. The range of motion around a joint.

Focused interval plan. A training approach that combines the benefits of a periodized plan and an interval training program.

Glycolytic pathway (glycolysis). The process of energy supply to the muscles during anaerobic work.

Heatherize. The process of economizing movement and implementing specific body positions in that movement, in most cases making it more efficient (though, in some cases, less effective).

Highball boulder problem. A boulder problem that usually involves going higher than the climber is willing to fall. While no actual measurement of height is officially given, the idea is that anything above fifteen feet is getting highball.

Interval training. The form of training that allows for the incorporation of the various elements of climbing in a more flexible pattern than the periodized training approach.

Isometric contraction. A muscle contraction in a way that simply holds tension, without a change in muscle length.

Jug. A handhold that is large enough for the climber to use the whole hand on the hold. This term is relative to the ability of the climber. Thus, some 5.14 climbers would consider a particular hold to be a jug, whereas a 5.11 climber would consider that some hold to be smaller than a jug.

Kinesiology. The study of the anatomic and mechanical basis for movement in sport. Various components of kinesiology include physiology, applied anatomy, and biomechanics.

Lactic acid. The by-product of the anaerobic breakdown of ATP to ADP. When oxygen is not present to oxidize pyruvic acid, the pyruvic acid changes into lactic acid. Some sports scientists consider lactic acid to be the cause of muscle soreness.

Mesomorphic. A body type that is very muscular.

Mitochondria. Referred to as the powerhouses of cells because of their ability to process oxygen within the cell.

Momentum. A force combining strength and dynamic energy.

Muscle bundle. A group of muscle cells. A number of bundles make up a whole muscle. Each bundle receives neurological messages and blood supply separately from other bundles.

Muscle fiber. A single muscle cell. Multiple fibers make up bundles, and bundles make up the muscle.

Neurological messages. The signals that are sent to and from the brain to the rest of the body and that provoke change. For example, a neurological message concerning pain signals from the pain receptors on the skin is transmitted to the brain. The brain then processes the signal and sends a neurological message to the muscle to take the area expressing pain and remove it from the object causing the pain.

On-sight. Climbing a route for the first time and not falling, without having been given any previous information concerning the route.

Open skill. A skill that is executed in an unpredictable environment. For example, basketball players execute skills in a constantly changing scenario.

Overtraining. Training to the point that you plateau in performance, experience an overuse injury, or begin to see a decline in performance regardless of increased rest time. Overtraining can also create symptoms of general fatigue with sleeplessness.

Overuse injury. Repetition of the same movements continuously can lead to an overuse injury. This results from continual strain to the tendons surrounding a joint.

Oxygen debt. The additional oxygen that is consumed during recovery from exercise in a given rest period.

Passive flexibility. The range of motion around a joint with the help of a resistive force (such as a partner) pushing against the limb to increase the range. Gravity also creates passive flexibility.

Performance goals. Goals that outline the performance or routes you wish to accomplish.

Periodized plan. A climbing schedule that allows for the training of all the elements of climbing in a structured and progressive manner. This approach is beneficial in seeing continued progress during your training process.

Pilates. A form of body work designed to assist in overall flexibility and strength.

Plateau. A point where there has been no change in performance over a substantial period of time.

PNF (proprioceptive neuromuscular feedback) stretching. This means that the muscle is elongated and then applies an isometric contraction (there is no change in the muscle length). At the completion of the stretch, the range is increased.

Power (powerful). The rate at which muscular strength is applied in movement. Power is usually defined by force over time. In climbing, power is considered to be short, difficult problems of only eight or fewer moves. The difficulty is great enough that an inability to apply the appropriate force results in failure.

Power endurance. The ability to combine strength and endurance, a form of work demanded by routes with many difficult moves. The response is to eventually reach the anaerobic threshold.

Pump. A sensation caused by anaerobic climbing without a rest. The forearms feel constricted and enlarged. The hands want to open up, and the climber has difficulty preventing this response.

Recovery. The ability of the body to return to normal heart rate after exercise. This includes the replenishment of the oxygen debt and return to normal blood pressure.

Recruitment. The simultaneous incorporation of muscle fibers in the contraction of the muscle. The greater the recruitment, the more force in the contraction.

Redpoint. To successfully climb a route on lead, without falling, after practice or rehearsal of the required sequence.

Rolfing. A form of body work designed to improve the structural alignment and potential energy of the body.

Sequence. The series of movements planned to climb a route.

Static strength. The maximal exertion of force from the muscles while in slow, continuous movement.

Stretch reflex. The cessation of a muscle contraction in response to a level of tension greater than any level the muscle has previously experienced. This is a safety mechanism to prevent muscle strain and injury.

Trauma injury. An unexpected injury caused by a sudden experience as opposed to a continual or repetitive action.

Transition. The movement between two stationary or resting positions, such as that between two climbing holds.

Undertraining. Not practicing a skill sufficiently to see improvement.

Visualize (visualization). Imagining yourself on the route and executing the necessary movements for success. The process of visualization is recommended in sport because of the mental rehearsal of the required arousal and memory of the sequence. It is also been shown that visualization excites the appropriate muscles for the exercise.

VO_2 max. The maximal ability to breathe in, transfer O_2 to the blood, and transport and utilize the oxygen by the working muscle.

References

Bannister, P., and P. Foster. 1986. Upper limb injuries associated with rock climbing. *British Journal of Sports Medicine* 20 (20): 55.

Benningfield, Phillip. 1999. *Colorado Bouldering*. Boulder, Colo.: Sharp End Publishing.

Berry, M., and D. Hamrick. 1980. Flexibility as an aid to climbing technique. *Off Belay* 52:13–15.

Bollen, S. R. 1988. Soft tissue injury in extreme rock climbers. *British Journal of Sports Medicine* 22 (4): 145–47.

Bollen, S. R., and C. K. Gunson. 1990. Hand injuries in competition climbers. *British Journal of Sports Medicine* 24 (1): 16–18.

Brown, D. A., and W. C. Miller. 1998. Normative data for strength and flexibility of women throughout life. *European Journal of Applied Physiology* 78:77–82.

Canadian Society for Exercise Physiology. 1993. *Certified Fitness Appraiser Resource Manual*. Toronto: Canadian Society for Exercise Physiology.

Cash, Mel. 1996. *Sport massage & remedial massage therapy*. London: Ebury Press.

Dawson, B., M. Fitzsimons, S. Green, C. Goodman, M. Carey, and K. Cole. 1998. Changes in performance, muscle metabolites, enzymes and fiber types after short sprint training. *European Journal of Applied Physiology* 78:163–69.

Goddard, D., and U. Neumann. 1993. *Performance Rock Climbing*. Mechanicsburg, Pa.: Stackpole Books.

Gresham, N. 1998. Training to failure is failing to train: Interval training for anaerobic endurance. *Climbing*, 15 June, 154–57.

Hamilton, E. M. N., and E. N. Whitney. 1983. *Concepts and Controversies in Nutrition*. 2d ed. St. Paul, Minn.: West.

Hardy, L., and K. Martindale. 1982. Some physiological parameters in rock-climbing. *Physical Education Review* 5 (1): 41–44.

Hawley, J., F. Brouns, and A. Jeukendrup. 1998. Strategies to enhance fat utilization during exercise. *Sport Medicine Journal* 25 (4): 241–54.

Horrigan, Joseph, and Jerry Robinson. 1991. *The 7-minute Rotator Cuff Solution*. Los Angeles: Health for Life.

Huang, Chungliang Al, and Jerry Lynch. 1992. *Thinking Body, Dancing Mind: TaoSports for Extraordinary Performance in Athletics, Business and Life*. New York: Bantam Books.

Kapit, Wynn, Robert Macey, and Esmail Meisami. 1987. *The Physiology Coloring Book*. New York: HarperCollins.

Leavitt, R. 1996. Lean and leaner is for dumb and dumber. *Climbing*, 15 December, 132–35.

Long, John. 1989. *How to rock climb*. Evergreen, Colo.: Chockstone Press.

———. 1991. *How to Rock Climb: Face Climbing*. Evergreen, Colo.: Chockstone Press.

Mace, Roger. 1979. Physiological arousal in climbers. *Physical Education Review* 2 (2): 141.

Maitland, M. 1992. Injuries associated with rock climbing. *Journal of Orthopaedic and Sports Physical Therapy* 16 (2): 68–73.

McNaughton, L., B. Dalton, and J. Tarr. 1998. The effects of creatine supplementation on high-intensity exercise performance in elite performers. *European Journal of Applied Physiology* 78:236–40.

Mileski, J. 1996. Rest assured: Head jams, shoulder scums and other resting tactics. *Climbing*, 1 November, 136–41.

Morgan, L. 1996. Upwardly mobile: Expert advice on taking it to the next level. *Climbing*, 15 September, 136–39.

Nakao, M., Y. Inoune, and H. Murakami. 1995. Longitudinal study of the effect of high intensity weight training on aerobic capacity. *European Journal of Applied Physiology* 70:20–25.

Oopik, V., M. Paaksuke, T. Sikku, S.Timmpman, L. Medijainen, J. Ereline, T. Smirnova, and E. Gapejeva. 1996. The effect of rapid weight loss on metabolism and isokinectic performance capacity: A case study of two well trained wrestlers. *Journal of Sports Medicine and Physical Fitness* 36:127–31.

Pederson, B. K., T. Rohde, and M. Zacho. 1996. Immunity in athletes. *Journal of Sports Medicine and Physical Fitness* 36:236–45.

Reynolds, Heather. 1995. Physical characteristics including strength, flexibility and body anthropometry of sport climbers at the recreational and elite levels. Thesis, Dalhousie University, Halifax, Nova Scotia.

Roy, Steven, and Richard Irvin. 1983. *Sports medicine: Prevention, evaluation, management, and rehabilitation.* Englewood Cliffs, N.J.: Prentice Hall.

Russum, W. 1989. Physiological determinants of rock climbing ability. Master's thesis, San Jose University.

Scott, C. B. 1997. Interpreting energy expenditure for anaerobic exercise and recovery: An anaerobic hypothesis. *Journal of Sports Medicine and Physical Fitness* 37:18–23.

Smith, Craig. 1997. Shrewd Food: Are you wasting money on risky diets and unproven supplements? *Climbing*, 1 August, 134–38.

Springer-Verlag. 1994. *European Journal of Applied Physiology and Occupational Physiology* 69:140–46.

Tomaczak, R. L., W. M. Wilshire, J. W. Lane, and D. C. Jones. 1989. Injury patterns in rock climbers. *Journal of Osteopathic Sports Medicine* 3 (2): 11–16.

Tortora, Gerard J. 1983. *Principles of human anatomy.* 3d ed. New York: Harper & Row.

Tsintzas, K., and C. Williams. 1998. Human muscle glycogen metabolism during exercise. *Sport Medicine Journal* 25 (1): 7–21.

Vivianni, F., and M. Calderan. 1991. The somatotype in a group of "top" free-climbers. *Journal of Sports Medicine and Physical Fitness* 31 (4): 581–86.

Wakasa, M. Get a grip: Do better climbers have stronger hands? *Rock & Ice* 80:43.

Watts, P., D. T. Martin, and S. Durtschi. 1993. The anthropometric profiles of elite male and female competitive sport rock climbers. *Journal of Sport Sciences* 11:113–17.

Watts, P., J. Newbury, and J. Sulentic. 1996. Acute changes in handgrip strength, endurance and blood lactate with sustained sport rock climbing. *Journal of Sports Medicine and Physical Fitness* 36:255–60.